DESIGN BROOKLYN

RENOVATION   RESTORATION INNOVATION INDUSTRY

ANNE HELLMAN

PHOTOGRAPHS BY MICHEL ARNAUD

STEWART, TABORI & CHANG   NEW YORK

Preface ANNE HELLMAN

WHEN I MOVED TO BROOKLYN SIXTEEN YEARS AGO, it felt like an outpost of Manhattan; now in many ways Brooklyn is its own center. Back then, friends had to make an effort to visit me, as did I if I wanted to join them "in the city" on the weekends. But the longer I lived here, the less time I spent in Manhattan, and the more inspired I became to get to know Brooklyn better.

When I was in my twenties and living in Williamsburg, new bars and restaurants were opening every month. An entire neighborhood changed before my eyes, from a desolate warehouse district to a vibrant art and music scene. This has taken place throughout Brooklyn in the past few decades: a new wave of artists, writers, musicians, and people of all professions has moved into the borough and made it a destination in its own right.

From Williamsburg to Boerum Hill to Carroll Gardens and finally to Cobble Hill, I made my way from home to home. Each of these neighborhoods, like all of Brooklyn's communities, has something unique to offer. My family's quest was to find a home where we could raise our children, and this is a common theme in Brooklyn. For many others the search is for a place where they can put down roots as small businesses, because workspaces as well as storefronts are more attainable here than in Manhattan. No matter what the pursuit is, with each new inhabitant an old building is kept alive—at least, that is the goal in a place with so much history. Each new business, each new home leaves an impression on these structures and their surroundings. Brooklyn is regenerating at a rapid rate, producing new art, new design, new cuisine, and new ideas for environmental living.

As I and the other members of this book's team—Michel Arnaud and Jane Creech—began our research into new Brooklyn design, there were multiple facets that could be focused upon, from wall art and ironwork, to public spaces and private gardens, to townhouse structure and new construction. There were also countless neighborhoods to explore, each one with its own spirit and sense of origin. We set out to discover as many new design happenings as we could in as many different neighborhoods as possible and found breathtaking new green architecture, such as the Brooklyn Botanic Garden Visitor Center and Sunset Park Materials Recycling Facility, dozens of innovative townhouse renovations and sustainable rooftop gardens, preeminent Brooklyn entities such as the Brooklyn Navy Yard and the Brooklyn Academy of Music, and many historic restorations, such as Fort Greene Park, made possible by generous gifts of time and effort. Although the resulting book does not, and probably could not, include all of these new spaces and ideas, the aim is to represent a full range.

Having lived here awhile, I was not as surprised by the sheer number of design innovations occurring everywhere in Brooklyn as I was by how interconnected they all were. To us, this signaled a much more important movement. Each designer we contacted generously linked us to another, so that soon we had a web of Brooklyn designers, architects, builders, and artisans to explore. Just as each neighborhood has a distinct cultural identity and design "bones" (some more apparent than others), the work of the designers and artists living and creating in these neighborhoods has its own distinct style and voice. Brooklyn's model creative community—supported by different styles and expressions side by side—is as inspiring as it is boundless. And its work has only just begun.

Design Brooklyn explores recent architectural and interior designs, from the spectacular to the everyday, throughout the borough. The gallery section offers a visual tour of Brooklyn: its bridges, its promenades, its wall art and markets, its one and only Coney Island. The chapters feature public spaces, private homes, and local restaurants and bars, as well as parks and gardens. Chapter 1, "Renovation," looks at combinations of old and new—not just preserving the old, but renewing with modern improvements such as the conversion of a factory building into the popular Wythe Hotel in Williamsburg and residences that put a fresh spin on Victorian interiors with mid-century furniture and contemporary wall coverings. This is followed by "Restoration," which discovers homes, a public park, and Jane's Carousel, all meticulously returned to their original states, showing how careful architectural preservation can thrive next to structures exploring more contemporary ideas. Chapter 3, "Innovation," reveals some of the most cutting-edge moves in architecture and design, from the BAM Fisher to avant-garde interior designs like Roberta's in Bushwick, composed with unconventional materials. The final chapter, "Industry," shows the breadth of Brooklyn's budding small-scale urban manufacturing, beginning in the Brooklyn Navy Yard and reaching out to designers' studios in other postindustrial areas.

Brooklyn design has become its own phenomenon, far-reaching and distinct. It is bound to invigorate and inspire anyone—anywhere.

AN INTERVIEW WITH MIKE D

AH: I have to ask: When the Beastie Boys wrote "No Sleep Till Brooklyn," what were your inspirations for the song at the time?

MIKE D: We were sitting around at an apartment I had in the West Village—and that's what we would do, sit around and write lyrics every night—and it just seemed like one of the funniest things we could come up with at the time. Then it quickly evolved into this kind of tour story, kind of a fantasy about being on tour and then getting back home to Brooklyn.

As a band, we started here in Brooklyn, on the top floor of the Yauchs' townhouse [in Brooklyn Heights]. And that's where we started playing and practicing. It's funny because if his parents were not crazy enough to let us actually play music on the top floor of their house, I don't think any of it would have been possible. As long as it was after school and before dinner, we could make a racket.

AH: Now that you live in Brooklyn, what do you think has changed about it since your school days in Brooklyn Heights? What's the same?

MIKE D: In a lot of ways, Brooklyn Heights is similar. Cobble Hill in certain ways is similar but also vastly different. You had two things. One, in the early seventies, there was this homesteading move-ment—Adam's parents were definitely part of it; his dad is an archi-tect—in which these younger artists, architects, and other urban profes-sionals, instead of just getting an apartment in Manhattan or moving to the suburbs with kids, would come to Brooklyn and renovate a town-house, in many cases reconfigur-ing these buildings *back* into the single-family homes they once were before being chopped up into small and cheap units. It had this ideal-ist quality to it. And then second, Brooklyn was a lot rougher and more dangerous. But Manhattan also was rougher then. You couldn't park a car on the street, or you could but you'd have to expect that everything inside of it would get stolen.

What has been lost in Manhattan is the sense of this playground for different people from all over the world who always wanted to immigrate to New York to be artists, writers, musicians, to express themselves on some level. Manhattan is now

basically off-limits due to the high
cost of living. I think Brooklyn in
a lot of ways has picked up that
slack.

AH: **What role did design play in your
early life?**

MIKE D: Growing up, my mom was an
interior designer and my father was
an art dealer, so I think it's in my
DNA. I've always considered it normal to be very conscious and aware
of every aesthetic decision. It's
the combination of having grown up
with the idea being front and center in my household that all of that
was relevant information, and that
my ideas in those areas mattered. I
would go to the Museum of Modern Art
and say, I like this, or, I don't
like that. I thought that was just
what you do—I didn't know any better. I had all this visual input all
the time.

Then, as a musician and band
member, a lot of it was about aesthetic representation. Obviously,
the music had to be there first, but
there's so much that goes along with
it and we were never a band that
handed off any of that. We always
collaborated or controlled very
closely every aesthetic process,
whether it was album covers, photographs, designing tour production
videos, films, whatever. I always
thought of that as the normal way to

do things because of how I was
brought up, which was kind of a
great thing. It was the same when
doing this house.

AH: **What were your criteria for designing
your townhouse? Your wife, Tamra Davis,
said that you wanted to move away from
the mid-century modern pieces you had
in your previous home.**

MIKE D: Mid-century design is interesting to look at as a jumping-off
point, for inspiration. The creators
of it were visionaries themselves.
But now there's a new generation
of designers, furniture makers, and
artists here who are informed by
that but have a new take.

We didn't have an agenda to move
to Brooklyn and only use Brooklyn
purveyors, but it took place as
we went along. It makes things a
lot easier when you're going a few
blocks to Red Hook to source really
great things.

AH: **When designing the Brooklyn Toile
wallpaper with Flavor Paper (in Boerum
Hill, see pages 80 and 239), how did
you decide which Brooklyn symbols you
wanted to appear in the pattern?**

MIKE D: The wallpaper was something
that we had talked about in terms
of the "townhouse vernacular"; it's
something you see all the time. But
then, how do you take this period
vernacular and have some fun with
it and update it? We went over
to Flavor Paper, which is right
around the corner, and they had a
Chinatown Toile. We asked them, Why
don't you have a Brooklyn Toile?
Then the lightbulb went off, and it
seemed like a really simple idea.
I thought, "I'll Google Image some
things, copy and paste, and it'll be

real easy." But then I realized that I have the ideas but am really out of my depth to execute this.

I worked with my friend, designer Vincent J. Ficarra at Revolver New York, and we realized that in order to do it right, we would have to hand-illustrate the whole thing. It was a labor of love because in this day and age, designers never get to draw anymore. They're only working in Photoshop. We did a lot of research. I never thought I would be spending time looking at books of Laura Ashley. Tamra was staying in Paris in a hotel where there was all this matching toile in the room and she took some photographs.

We felt that we could play with the iconography but then configure it to the structure. There's a formula for toile. You have to have pleasant nature scenes, although a lot of times in toile they involve hunting. But birds, fine—Brooklyn, we have pigeons [laughs], we have native foliage. We took the Nathan's hot dog and put that in the clouds.

I picked the iconography of Brooklyn—the mom with the stroller, the guy with the bike chain around his waist. I'd be driving through Williamsburg and see a pack of Hasidic guys and be trying to grab my iPhone to take a picture, thinking, That's it! That's what we need.

AH: **How do you think design relates to your music?**

MIKE D: I think the correlation is very much in the implementation, because what we learned as a band is basically that with any artistic endeavor there's making it good and then there's the aspiration of trying to make it great. So it's the idea of not being afraid to hold on to your vision and fighting for it, and then all the sacrifices you have to make of putting in all the extra work, of having to actually implement that. Because it's fine and well to say, Okay, we know what we want, but then what makes those things really good is the attention to all the detail. If you were doing it just as a business you'd say, Look we don't have the time. Just cut this and cut that and it's fine. That was something that we learned together. I also feel like I was taught that from Adam Yauch in our band, because he was a year older but he innately had the tireless energy to focus. That applies to this house, because there are so many things that you have to fight for and tirelessly oversee.

AH: **In making any kind of art, you need a sense of elements working together, as in design. How do you think design connects to other art forms?**

MIKE D: Well, it's experiential. Music is experiential, art is experiential. Design, architecture, those are all things that are experiences. And I guess in that sense I'm always the most fascinated by things that operate on that level. Brooklyn is again a good example. You look at it in the last few years and it's become a breeding ground for all of these experiential realms. Whether it's food—there are chefs who may have worked at some of the best restaurants in Manhattan, but when they want the freedom of really expressing themselves and being able to do it on their own, where are they going to open up a restaurant? Here, because it's more affordable and they can get more idiosyncratic and genuine in their expression and more free of compromise, which is necessary in Manhattan because you've got this ridiculous overhead.

AH: **Besides affordability, why do you think Brooklyn inspires this kind of place where artists and designers can branch out on their own and express themselves?**

MIKE D: This is a fortuitous time in Brooklyn in particular. The New York that I grew up in, in my early adolescence—which I have a real fondness for because I feel as though I was raised in a large part by that lawless, openly creative New York City—now because of the economic changes and the homogenization that has occurred in Manhattan, it's largely devoid of so many of those factors. Brooklyn opened up that home for designers, artists, fabricators, creative people of all sorts, whether it's Red Hook or Bushwick.

I think it's the sense of community that Brooklyn is able to have that Manhattan is a little too chaotic and dense to have. It is a home for creativity, but I think what all these people value about being here and living here and working here and having Brooklyn as part of their identity is that there is a sense of community. When we moved into this house, the neighbors to the left and to the right of us both came over the day we moved in with a bottle of Prosecco and said, Welcome to the neighborhood. Having lived in many, many different places in Manhattan, that's never, ever happened to me.

Brooklyn somehow, even though we are part of New York City and even though we are all of a ten-minute train ride from Lower Manhattan, we still have a tighter sense of community and a slightly more relaxed pace, which allows this sense of community to happen. In Brooklyn you have that access—to neighbors, designers, builders—that allows you to refine things and to really collaborate.

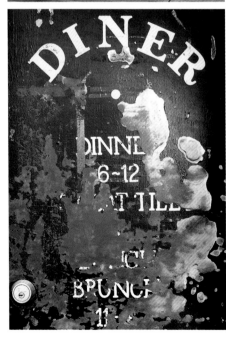

W. H. AUDEN
POET (1907 - 1973)

LIVED IN BROOKLYN HEIGHTS FROM 1939 TO 1941.
FROM 1939 TO 1940 ON THE TOP FLOOR OF THIS HOUSE,
WHERE HE WROTE "NEW YEAR LETTER."

"AND LOVE ILLUMINATES AGAIN
THE CITY AND THE LION'S DEN,
THE WORLD'S GREAT RAGE, THE TRAVEL OF YOUNG MEN."

THE W. H. AUDEN SOCIETY, JUNE 29, 1990

INTRODUCTION

Innovation in Context: A Brief History of Brooklyn

Lucas G. Rubin

A little before six p.m. on the evening of May 28, 1880, a fire broke out in the engine room of the Union Packing Box Factory on Brooklyn's Front Street. Given the density of flammable materials stored within, the building was a total loss even before the first fire engines arrived. When the smoke cleared, the factory and several other establishments—including a brass-finishing studio, paint works, soap manufacturer, and coal dealer—were almost completely destroyed.[1]

The owner of the box factory, James H. Dykeman, took the $30,000 he received in insurance compensation and promptly relocated his business to the Gowanus Canal district, one of Brooklyn's burgeoning industrial zones. The revived company soon prospered, and over the years Dykeman moved the plant to increasingly larger quarters. In 1899-1900 he built an extensive complex adjacent to the canal, from which barges could offload lumber next to the factory and carry away completed boxes.[2] The structure was proudly emblazoned with Dykeman's name—a profound statement of the fulfillment of one man's American dream, and a reflection of the opportunity, dynamism, and energy of the age. In many ways, Dykeman's Brooklyn prefigured that of the borough in the early twenty-first century: dynamic, vibrant, and innovative. From the hip neighborhoods of Williamsburg and Fort Greene to stroller-friendly Park Slope and along the cobblestone streets of a revitalized waterfront district (christened Dumbo, for Down Under the Manhattan Bridge Overpass, in the late 1970s), the borough is considered one of the most exciting and desirable places to live. It is also home to a diverse collection of artists, professionals, and entrepreneurs, whose energy and creativity are manifest in the myriad studios, boutique shops, and small businesses that now call Brooklyn home.

This passion for innovation, invention, and creativity has long characterized Brooklyn's history; in many ways it has been its defining ethos.

But change has also been central to Brooklyn's history—and not necessarily change as in gradual evolution and transition, but rather drastic, large-scale, and sometimes rapid transformation: from rich to

---

1. "Fierce Flames in Brooklyn," *New York Times*, May 28, 1880, 2.
2. *Real Estate Record and Builders' Guide* 63, no. 1609 (January 14, 1899), 88; and *The Disston Crucible: A Magazine for the Millman* 3, no. 6 (July 15, 1914), 89-91.

ABOVE The National Packing Box Factory, built by James H. Dykeman in 1899 and renamed from its predecessor, still stands today on the corner of Nevins and Union Streets near the Gowanus Canal. It is the site of Proteus Gowanus, a gallery and reading space.

poor (and back again), from sparsely to densely populated, and from agrarian to industrial (and with its green initiatives, some might say "and back again"). Each of these phases, in turn, has left its own indelible mark on the urban fabric of Brooklyn.

The Canarsee were the last of the indigenous peoples to call Brooklyn home. A branch of the Lenape people, they lived in a number of scattered settlements and subsisted on fishing, hunting, and gathering. Other than remains brought to light through archaeology, they have left few indications of their presence—save the eponym of the Canarsie neighborhood and the routes of Flatbush Avenue and Kings Highway.

The first Europeans to settle Brooklyn were the Dutch who, beginning in the 1630s, established a constellation of villages across the southwestern tip of Long Island. By 1661, there were six such centers: Breuckelen (roughly modern Brooklyn Heights and the origin of Brooklyn's name), New Amersfoort (Flatlands),

Midwout (Flatbush), New Utrecht (part of Bensonhurst), Boswick (Bushwick), and the lone English settlement of Gravesend, settled by Lady Deborah Moody in 1645 as an Anabaptist refuge. Ferry service to New York City began in the 1640s, setting the foundation for their intermingled economies—and anticipating their eventual merger. Even now, embedded within the urban matrix of Brooklyn, are remains of this earlier time: surviving Dutch toponyms (such as Bergen, Wyckoff, and Van Brunt Streets), the extant street grid of Lady Moody's original settlement, and some sixteen early Dutch-American farmhouses scattered throughout the borough. Even the word *stoop*—an architectural feature that virtually defines Brooklyn—comes from the Dutch word of the same meaning, *stoep*. Perhaps some small part of Brooklyn's pioneering spirit might also be due to its Dutch heritage.

In 1664, the area fell under English rule. When the colonies erupted in revolt a little more than a century later, one of the most

4-28

A relic of Brooklyn's Dutch past. Begun c. 1652, the Pieter Claesen Wyckoff House is probably the oldest standing building in New York City. The Wyckoff family owned the house until 1901, though later descendants reacquired the property in 1961. Landmarked in 1965, it has been a museum since 1982.

significant battles of the war was fought in Brooklyn on August 27, 1776. It was an unmitigated disaster, and a seven-year occupation by the British followed immediately thereafter. Reminders of the revolutionary period are still present in the borough, most notably the Prison Ship Martyrs' Monument in Fort Greene Park and Park Slope's Old Stone House, which was originally a Dutch farmhouse (though it's since been rebuilt and moved slightly) and the location of the 1st Maryland Regiment's valiant efforts to cover George Washington's retreat over the Gowanus Creek.

Following the war, the town of Brooklyn (i.e., the original settlement next to the East River, now going by the anglicized version of its name) grew rapidly and, with the opening of the Fulton Steam Ferry in 1814, became the world's first commuter suburb, as residents working in New York City traveled daily from their Brooklyn homes.

The town also began to grow beyond its original boundaries, absorbing a number of adjacent settlements in the process—and leading to its incorporation as a city in 1834. Around the same time, to the immediate north, other areas began coalescing into larger polities. Williamsburg became its own city in 1852—only to be annexed (along with

Bushwick) by greater Brooklyn a mere three years later.

Given its excellent harborage and access, by the 1850s and 1860s the Brooklyn waterfront was lined with various industrial, manufacturing, and marine enterprises, a phenomenon accelerated by the demands of the Civil War. The Brooklyn Navy Yard, which opened in 1806, would build seventeen warships for the Union cause alone. Remains from this era also abound; in the waterfront neighborhood of Red Hook, for instance, surviving period warehouses cogently evince the Union's indomitable industrial might.

In addition to being an industrial powerhouse, Brooklyn was the Union's third largest city—and also one of President Lincoln's most loyal. As neighboring New York City was put to the torch during the 1863

The former National Packing Box Factory, built by James H. Dykeman in 1899, located at the corner of Nevins and Union Streets adjacent to the Gowanus Canal.

RIGHT The Teaser, Coney Island's Luna Park, June 13, 1911. To many, Coney Island is practically synonymous with Brooklyn. It was here that technology was married to recreation.

draft riot, the indefatigable Henry Ward Beecher railed against slavery and the Confederacy from his pulpit at Brooklyn Heights' landmark Plymouth Church.

Following the war came a number of significant developments: Prospect Park was completed (1867) and the first rail lines to Coney Island were laid. Both were areas dedicated to amusement and leisure, novel consequences borne, in part, of the surplus time made available through industrialization. Though each embodied a markedly different response—Calvert Vaux's masterpiece being one of refinement and splendor; Coney Island's, on the other hand, being one of technologically enhanced excitement, energy, and tawdriness—both provided elements critical to the formation of Brooklyn's topography and character.

In 1883, the Brooklyn Bridge opened, joining the nation's first and third largest cities. While the bridge itself became iconic, its impact on Brooklyn was profoundly transformative; now linked physically, the relationship between the two cities became more than symbiotic.

Up through the 1890s, Brooklyn continued to expand outward, gobbling up the last independent towns along the way. It was, however, also running out of energy—or, more accurately,

out of money. The city had grown so quickly that it had gone broke attempting to maintain and expand an already inadequate infrastructure; in short, it lacked the tax base of the neighboring metropolis. And so, on the first day of 1898, the consolidation of Brooklyn (as well as Queens, the Bronx, and Staten Island) with Manhattan occurred—though absorption by Manhattan might be a more accurate description.

Initially, much good came of consolidation: more capital was available, and in 1908, Brooklyn was connected to the single-fare subway system (the famous ferry, now superannuated, ceased service in 1924). There was, however, also the negative; most significantly, the "draw" of Manhattan (and later, the suburbs) fostered an exodus of affluent residents from the borough. This was further exacerbated in the wake of the Great Depression and, later, postwar deindustrialization. By the 1950s, many previously wealthy areas—such as Park Slope, Bedford-Stuyvesant, and Clinton Hill—had become quite poor. Many of the great old mansions were torn down, while once-elegant brownstones were divided into rooming houses and tenements. Commercial and manufacturing establishments closed, while abandoned and derelict buildings, in turn, multiplied. Most devastating

ABOVE A 1939 tax photo of a typical
brownstone block on 2nd Street in Park Slope.

to Brooklyn's psyche, however, was
the 1958 departure of the beloved
Dodgers for the greener pastures of
a thriving Los Angeles.

Beginning in the 1960s, however, the seeds were planted for
what would eventually blossom into
a wholesale renaissance. A slow
trickle of well-educated and more
prosperous residents began returning
to the borough.[3] Their reasons for
doing so were many—affordability and
space, for one—but many of the same
factors that had made Brooklyn so
desirable in the nineteenth century
were still present (if now somewhat
dormant): accessibility, proximity
to services, and aesthetic charm.

These pioneers (whose efforts
became known as the Brownstone
Revival Movement) slowly and system-
atically began to remake the borough. Their efforts yielded a string
of results: the establishment of the
Brooklyn Heights landmark district

(1965) and the (ongoing) reclamation
and revitalization of the housing
stock in a large number of neighborhoods. Though gentrification brought
its share of problems and social
upheavals, these new residents were
essentially bucking the national
trend of abandoning inner cities by
investing in the borough. By the
1990s, New York City was well on the
road to fiscal recovery, and at the
dawn of the twenty-first century,
Brooklyn's rightful place had been
restored.

Brooklyn's history has also been
defined by its remarkable diversity. As far back as Lady Moody's
Gravesend, some areas have been
characterized by the dominant eth-
nicity of their inhabitants, which,
like the greater borough, are in a
constant state of flux—an Italian
Bay Ridge, for instance, is giving away to an Arab one, as a once
Jewish (and Italian) Flatbush has
become a West Indian enclave. Within
neighborhoods, there are sometimes
fluid borders between different cultures and budding syncretic tra-
ditions, such as the emergence of
restaurants that serve more than one
type of ethnic cuisine (Chinese and
Spanish, for instance) or blended
musical styles (like Afro-Semitic).

Along with change and diversity
has come a drive for entrepreneur-
ship and artistry—a disposition
that connects a nineteenth-century
entrepreneur like Dykeman with his
modern-day counterparts. Though some
of these are remembered by name—
Pratt or Litchfield, for instance—
most have been forgotten, their only
legacy the brownstones, factories,
warehouses, and stores that they've

3. For more on the Brownstone Revival Movement, see Suleiman Osman's terrific tome, *The Invention of Brownstone Brooklyn: Gentrification and the Search for Authenticity in Postwar New York* (New York: Oxford University Press, 2011).

left behind. These, in turn, have come to define Brooklyn's very fabric. Given the solidity of their construction and the enduring aesthetics of their basic design, they also provide the palette upon which successive generations have impressed their own ideas and energies.

The denouement of Dykeman's old box factory and the next life of the company's buildings clearly demonstrates this. While Dykeman's company remained successful through the first two decades of the twentieth century, its fortunes began to wane and the firm leased underutilized space to other entities. A devastating fire in 1932 brought about the demise of the company in 1936.[4] By the 1950s, the Gowanus area had become a desolate, depopulated wasteland, the canal itself heavily polluted. Parts of the old factory were utilized by a number of transient companies, such as the A. Barone Toy Manufacturing Company, while other portions lay unused. Then, in the 1980s, the old building was divided up and converted into artists' studios. It has since become home to Proteus Gowanus, an interdisciplinary gallery and reading room, named after Proteus, a Greek god personified by his everchanging shape.[5] The appellation is appropriate not just for the organization, but for the building itself, which has seen so many changes in use and function.

It might be an appropriate metaphor for Brooklyn, as well.

Like Paris's Left Bank or Rome's Trastevere, modern Brooklyn—especially its Victorian-era brownstone belt—

possesses its own unique bohemian identity. But unlike them, it contains the infrastructure of an entirely independent city: a seat of government, downtown business district, waterfront, and manufacturing areas, as well as a broad range of diverse cultural institutions. The neighborhoods beyond the brownstone belt are home to their own separate, vital, and distinct communities, some of them semi-suburbanized. Though unique unto themselves, they too share the same pioneering spirit of change, diversity, and innovation.

These attributes—change, diversity, and innovation—have permitted Brooklyn to reinvent itself along the way, and are very much at the heart of its current renaissance.

4. Dorothy Miner et al., *Gowanus Canal Corridor*, Columbia University, M.S. Historic Preservation Program, Studio II (Spring 2008), 31.

5. http://proteusgowanus.org/about (accessed September 22, 2012).

The word *renovation* is particularly suited to Brooklyn, a place that has kept much of the old architecture from both its industrial and its residential pasts, and has, in recent years, welcomed top thinkers and creative people from around the world to accomplish new work on its soil. All eyes have turned toward architects, designers, and craftspeople in the borough to glean ideas for bridging the old and the new in objects and interiors.

Especially in Brooklyn, home renovation can mean a new approach to an old problem. Architects and homeowners have developed better solutions for light-challenged interiors and for juxtaposing the original building with new construction and a modern aesthetic. Others have conceived of fresh modes of interactivity for vertical living so that families can live and work at home in a more balanced way, and some simply enliven their Victorian rooms with fresh coats of white or black paint or insert contemporary furnishings.

In Boerum Hill, a defunct belt factory transforms into a bustling arts center. The Wythe Hotel in Williamsburg has become a beacon of its day, reinventing an industrial-era cooperage into a singularly Brooklyn hotel. Designers like those from the studio Nightwood give the bones of old furniture new life and build with salvaged wood and handmade fabrics. Some business owners have retrofitted complete vintage looks from scratch, fashioning a bar or retail shop with utter care and attention to detail.

This is how Brooklyn is enjoying old buildings, objects, and processes: by collaging them into present-day aesthetics and functions.

1

RENOVATION

Vision in White 2ND STREET

ABOVE AND OPPOSITE
Built around 1900, this classic Park Slope brownstone maintains its original façade. The interior was almost entirely painted white, displaying original detailing in bright relief.

What Amy Gropp Forbes and Adam Forbes immediately loved about this Park Slope townhouse was that the interior—all of it, down to the details—had been painted white. The original woodwork remained intact; it simply looked different, more airy, than the other Victorian homes on the block. Coming from a loft in Manhattan, the couple thought the white interior provided just the right amount of modernity, and yet it still honored the elaborately carved moldings and trims instated a century earlier.

On first glance, the building needed little more than a cosmetic renovation, but as work began, more serious structural issues revealed themselves. Both the plumbing and the electrical wiring had to be redone, which meant the walls had to be opened up. Fortunately, architect David Sherman, a Park Slope resident himself, and the contractor knew how to protect the woodwork during construction.

"As we created new things we made an effort to mimic details in a slightly more pared-down way," says Amy. "We kept a certain level of detail so it wouldn't be too obvious where the renovation stopped and started, with one exception: the kitchen."

The major work required did allow the couple to make a big change to the traditional brownstone layout: they moved the kitchen upstairs to the third floor. The idea sprang from Adam's wish—he is also trained as an architect—to place the kitchen where there was more direct sunlight. In most townhouses, the kitchen is kept on the first (garden) or second (parlor) floor, for proximity to the backyard. This house, however, had only a shallow outdoor space in the back. And because there was an extension on the garden and parlor levels, there was opportunity for a generous terrace and outdoor dining area off a third-floor kitchen.

The result of this rearrangement is both practical and aesthetically pleasing. The parlor floor now has a gracious living room, sitting area, and formal dining room (a small kitchen next to the dining room comes in handy during larger dinner parties). Then, up one flight, a sun-filled family dining area and kitchen awaits, opening onto a deck and green space.

Six Forty Two

OPPOSITE AND ABOVE
In decorating the living
and dining rooms, Amy
Gropp Forbes could
realize an aesthetic
vision she had essentially
grown up with: her
father admired and
collected mid-century
modern furniture, while
her mother was a
craftsperson. Carrying
out this vision meant
balancing elaborate

details with a modern
sense of color. She
prefers neutral tones
and views color as
an accessory—the
bright bag that gives
a monochrome outfit
just a spark of intensity.
The original woodwork
gleams white in the
parlor rooms, upholding
the grandeur of the high-
ceilinged spaces as they
were first conceived.

RENOVATION / PARK SLOPE

Painting the carved-wood fireplace surround white brings the Victorian details into the twenty-first century. "I love the ornateness and floweriness of a design combined with a more subdued palette," Amy explains. "It's a big theme in the house overall."

LEFT Amy placed beautifully crafted pieces throughout the parlor rooms, including still lifes of cream-colored ceramic wares on tabletops and mantelpieces. She and Adam Forbes accented the white here and in the dining room with burnished bronze hardware. The electric-blue Eero Saarinen Womb chair and magenta and rattan daybed by Hans Wegner give the pale rooms a burst of color.

ABOVE A built-in glass-encased library spans one wall of the sitting room, with a writing desk that flips down from the center— all of which is original to the residence. The owners replicated the installation upstairs in the family dining room to hold dishware.

In the dining room, the coffered ceiling and wainscoting enrich the eye with a bit of opulence, yet the even tone of white keeps the room just minimal enough to feel contemporary. The owners found the Murano glass chandelier while traveling in Venice and were pleased with its unusually subdued color.

LEFT When tearing out the bathroom where they planned the new kitchen, Amy and Adam uncovered raw beams and brick and incorporated these rougher elements into the kitchen design, bringing a feel of the rustic as well as the minimal into the traditional brownstone interior. They designed all of the cabinetry to fit underneath deep countertops, keeping the painted-white brick walls bare, with only hooks for pots and pans.

BELOW Moving the kitchen to the third floor meant that the family could create a terrace on top of the extension, perfect for outdoor dining.

OPPOSITE The room adjoining the second-floor kitchen has an informal family dining table and orange molded-plastic Eames chairs.

A Retreat for All Seasons PROSPECT PLACE GARDEN

ABOVE AND OPPOSITE Mariza Scotch and Dièry Prudent have integrated aged wood and antique metal pieces throughout the garden, giving it a country feel. The iron wheels placed in the center were part of a large printing press that had been in the basement of the house.

Mariza Scotch and Dièry Prudent have something that is rare in any city, even in Brooklyn: a 100-foot-long garden. Built as part of an 1870s development, the house and backyard have undergone an extensive renovation by the owners, who worked with Matthew Baird of Baird Architects to remodel the kitchen on the garden and with Susan Welti of Foras Studio to design and landscape the yard. Scotch and Prudent found inspiration in the Noguchi Museum in Long Island City, for its color palette, spirit of repose, and simple beauty.

"When we purchased the house in 1996, the garden was a long, lush alley of green. We'd never seen anything like it in Brooklyn," says Scotch. "When winter came and the green disappeared, we started the long process of imagining a space we could enjoy seeing in all seasons."

Stepping out from the kitchen through glass doors, the first section provides an idyllic outdoor dining experience. In the middle of the garden, a gently raised wooden platform shaped around a white pine tree makes a good place for parties and events. Often Prudent, who is a physical trainer, uses it to teach exercise and yoga classes. In the back third of the garden, designer and builder Jeremy Seigle constructed a retractable workout apparatus, which easily disassembles to tuck under the platform. This way, Prudent can train clients during the day and then the space can be used at other times for entertaining.

Inside, the couple chose stainless steel for the kitchen cabinetry because it would wear well and they prefer to use authentic materials. "It made sense to fabricate everything locally and to keep the fridge, cabinetry, and shelving in a consistent surface and profile," explains Scotch. A large bluestone fireplace warms the dining area in the room. "One evening after meeting with our architect, we had an amazing dinner at Savoy (now closed), cooked entirely in the fireplace near our table. We fell in love with the idea of being able to create the experience at home."

A garden this large could very easily have wasted areas here and there, but this one is well thought out and used. Sitting in the kitchen, with the doors open, it seems as though the house itself continues on another hundred feet.

Scotch and Prudent worked with Foras Studio to design a three-part back garden, which measures 100 feet in length. A custom-designed table made out of a Corten steel base and ipe top adds subtle contrast to greenery most of the year.

LEFT Foras Studio commissioned Jeremy Seigle to custom build the outdoor dining table, which has a Corten steel base and ipe top.

BELOW Prudent is a personal trainer and had this workout structure built so that it could be dismantled and tucked under the wooden walkway.

ABOVE Wooden walk-
ways connect the three
areas of the long garden.
The large white pine
provides the middle area
with shade, creating
a separate space for
parties and events.

RIGHT A quiet bench
sits just outside the
kitchen. Prudent also
uses the middle platform
to train clients and
teach exercise classes.

LEFT The wood-burning fireplace keeps the space warm, both functionally and aesthetically. The stone surround is honed bluestone from New York State.

BELOW The kitchen, placed on the garden level, was carefully designed by Scotch and Prudent in collaboration with Matthew Baird. Scotch chose stainless steel for the cabinets and appliances, which were custom-made in New Jersey.

An indoor-outdoor potting room provides an area for storing al fresco necessities while keeping them dry in bad weather. Arne Jacobsen Ant chairs provide seating.

A Subtle Shift in Proportion 3RD STREET

ABOVE This 1890s brownstone was built as part of a row of four houses. Faces carved into the facade stonework most likely represent the first owners.

OPPOSITE Fogarty Finger opened up the rear extension with tall steel windows, connecting the parlor and garden floors to each other and to the backyard.

The state of an 1890s brownstone when purchased often determines the extent of the renovation that follows. Just as often, it is the decision to brighten the interior and make it more spacious that takes the lead. The owners of this Park Slope brownstone worked with architects Chris Fogarty and Robert Finger, of Fogarty Finger, to achieve a modern re-creation of a traditional Victorian townhouse.

Of the important architectural alterations that Fogarty Finger made, the "subtlest" change—reproportioning the parlor rooms—had the greatest effect. The owners wanted a large kitchen that was central, functional, and that participated in family life. After many discussions, the architects decided to shift the central dividing wall to give more depth to what would be the kitchen and dining room, shortening the front parlor.

"Adjusting to vertical living is understanding where to put the kitchen," says Finger. "If we were going to do the kitchen on the parlor floor, as opposed to on the garden, which is traditional, then we were going to do it on the scale of the other rooms." The kitchen is inherently modern, but the architects balanced it within the space, continuing the plaster molding around the room to blend it with the original architecture.

Glass doors open onto the garden from the family room, where the owners, who are from Puerto Rico, desired a space for afternoon barbecues and entertaining. "We wanted to show our mix of cultures, love for life and for color, and our love for Brooklyn, mixing industrial pieces with the nature outside in the garden," says one owner.

By moving the wall between the kitchen and formal living room forward about three feet toward the front of the house, the main stairwell was necessarily shortened, creating the challenge of how to gracefully compress the staircase. Finger developed the elegant shell-like shape for the stairs to make them more compact. The result is a singularly unique set of stairs—a blend of the traditional rectangular townhouse staircase and a spiral one running up all three floors and illuminated by an oval skylight.

ABOVE The kitchen is a crisp, minimalist presentation of a Caesarstone countertop, white lacquer cabinets, and dark walnut paneling, open to the formal dining room.

OPPOSITE Large steel windows on the dining room and narrow extension connect the kitchen-dining area to the garden.

Architect Robert Finger
designed an oval
staircase to fit the
new stairwell.

LEFT The owners worked closely with Fogarty Finger's in-house interior designer, Ana Luchangco, to select an Andrée Putman Crescent Moon Sofa, choosing a heavy woven Bergamo fabric for the back of the sofa, bound to be bumped into by the couple's children, and a smooth ocher-hued fabric for the seating side. The sofa pillows are by Bergamo.

RIGHT Mira Nakashima created a ten-seat dining table of American black walnut, and Brooklyn-based woodworker Eric Manigian custom built the dining chairs with blue cowhide seats. A David Weeks fixture hangs above the table, and a shag rug from Kea on Atlantic Avenue was converted into a wall tapestry.

Due to the shortening of the room, the architects were pleased to find that the original marble fireplace in the formal parlor was now centered on its wall. The 1940s Henry Klumb daybed from MondoCane is made of ebonized wood and hemp. Luchangco selected a Shadow rug in silver and gold silk and wool by Rug Art. The silver Gaetana Scolari chandelier has a stainless-steel finish that reflects the hues in the room.

ABOVE Nothing in the garden-level family room is meant to be precious. A coffee table fashioned out of a mining cart from France carries a thick, rounded, interlaminated glass top. A Bend sofa from B & B Italia in magenta fabric vibrates against the wallpaper, called Taurus, designed by artist Sarah Morris and made by Maharam. Luchangco added a 1960s Adesso Liceu de Arte Jacaranda chair. Kyle Bunting fabricated the custom Jet Stream-patterned cowhide rug, made from a combination of natural and dyed hides.

LEFT The extension itself becomes an open scissor stair between the two bottom floors, encouraging interactivity between the kitchen and family room below.

RIGHT A hanging light fixture over the bar table is made from reclaimed metal parts by Obsolete in California. Eric Manigian crafted the bar table.

RENOVATION / **PARK SLOPE**

The Interactive Vertical CHEEVER PLACE

ABOVE Cheever Place displays tidy rows of Greek Revival homes, built as part of Brooklyn's expansion south of Brooklyn Heights in the 1840s and 1850s. The four-story residences housed immigrant families who came to work on the docks in nearby Red Hook; often more than one family lived on each floor.

This one-block street, tucked between the main veins of Henry and Hicks Streets on the southern edge of Cobble Hill, has been home to generations of the same few families for more than a hundred years. The four-story row houses were typically divided up to hold a family on each floor, and sometimes more. When the owners of this Greek Revival home first came upon the property, the four stories had long been sectioned into apartments. Still, there was a glimmer of what it could be as a cohesive triplex and garden pied-à-terre for one owner's parents.

The building was unusually wide at twenty-three feet, and the owners wanted to know what the possibilities were. Jen and Roy Leone of Leone Design Studio, based in Gowanus, suggested a dramatic change to the center of the house: a cutout that would run next to the staircase, essentially bringing the volume of the skylight from the roof through the middle of the interior. This would transform the light conditions inside, and not much square footage would actually be missed, since the house was wider to begin with.

"We elected to take the space normally reserved for the hallway and remove it," says Jen Leone. "We then placed a series of semiprivate areas along this open vertical space." Although it was hard to imagine before construction, what Leone Design Studio ultimately created was a more interactive home, in which family members could speak to one another from different floors, the central opening providing connection rather than separation.

At the same time, it was important to the owners that the house possess a sense of its authentic Greek Revival self. Although there were no existing details to restore, the architects designed a vocabulary for the perimeter of the dwelling that referred to the historic detailing while accommodating the modern insertions the owners wanted to make. In this way, the tall parlor windows and added French doors off the back wear a more Greek Revival look, whereas areas in the center of the house are more modern.

The open vertical not only defines the interior; it transforms the typical townhouse stairwell into a point of communication with the rest of the home.

The fireplace in the parlor keeps to the Greek Revival style. Leone Design Studio fashioned a contemporary interpretation of crown molding and trim from the period. To lighten the rooms and maximize their ceiling height, they flipped the molding onto the ceiling. The gold-leaf Bubble chandelier is by Pelle.

ABOVE Standing underneath the skylight, looking up, it is almost possible to see the entire house at once.

LEFT The second-floor landing still has depth even with the hallway taken out. The skylight bathes the passageways in light even on cloudy days.

The notion of merging modern
and traditional aesthetics
carried over to the staircase,
which Leone Design Studio
gave a contemporary mix
of wood and black while
maintaining a traditional feel.
The cutout provides the ability
to correspond between different
levels, from parlor level to
master floor and all the way
up to the children's floor.

LEFT The central kitchen, open to the stairs, makes it easy to talk to guests while cooking, and to children playing on the third floor. The walnut wrap of the countertop is echoed in walnut built-ins throughout as well as in the stair banister. The Ripple rug is by Eskayel.

BELOW For entertaining, the owners desired a modern kitchen and dining area, which Leone Design Studio placed in the center of the parlor level facing the backyard and exposed to the staircase.

ARCHITECTS' VOICE:

JEN AND ROY LEONE

LEONE DESIGN STUDIO

There is a generational shift happening in Brooklyn right now. Many of these houses we are asked to renovate haven't been touched in thirty, forty, fifty years. That older generation is selling, so there is a change of hands to a new generation and with that an opportunity to alter and transform these houses for the next century.

Designing a townhouse in some ways is a great challenge for an architect, because given the shell there are so few opportunities to radically transform the house. And even though they are so similar, each one is a little bit different. In every project we do, we find that nobody wants to sacrifice square footage, even for a great move. But on Cheever Place, it was the loss of a very small piece that created such a huge gain.

One of the typical problems in a Brooklyn brownstone is the separation of the floors, what we call "pancake living." By opening up the staircase, what we get is a flow of space where the parents can communicate with the kids upstairs, and the kids can call down to Mom or Dad in the kitchen—a series of moments where everyone can see and talk to one another. It creates connectivity in a way that is usually impractical in a Brooklyn brownstone.

Meadow on High

CLINTON STREET ROOFTOP GARDEN

OPPOSITE Landscape designer Julie Farris bordered the ipe pathway with one- and two-inch Mexican river stones. An outdoor grill and refrigerator nestle against the reconceived bulkhead, which provides light to the modern townhouse below with a glass door and window.

RIGHT The roof retreat has breathtaking views of Brooklyn and Manhattan beyond. Farris installed recessed Bega lighting in the walls around the seating and grass areas and inserted Jesco pin lights along one side of the wooden path to create a subtle glow at night. The dining table and lounge furniture are from Teak Warehouse. Farris found the retractable umbrella at Room & Board.

Inspired by Piet Oudolf's plantings on Manhattan's High Line, landscape designer Julie Farris created a rooftop respite for her home in Cobble Hill that can withstand the elements and provide a pleasant space for al fresco dining and relaxation. Farris conceived of the garden in two parts: a square patch of artificial grass where her children can play and a deck for lounging and dining. A wide ipe pathway joins the two areas, giving a sense of definition as well as connection.

Farris chose a hardy plant palette that is drought and wind tolerant. She wanted a more wild look in the middle bed, which she planted directly onto the waterproof roof membrane using a layered green-roof system—a root barrier, drainage mat, Styrofoam, and filter fabric for proper drainage. The meadow effect she created keeps the deck lively and colorful rather than overly manicured, and balances the square of cropped green grass and the crisp lines of the ipe elements throughout.

ABOVE Farris had the
High Line in Manhattan
in mind when she
designed her roof deck
and garden.

ABOVE Grasses and
wildflowers enjoy the
sun and were chosen
for their durability. Farris
combined calamagrostis,
molinia, nepeta, achil-
lea, monarda, dianthus,
wild geraniums, and
wild strawberries in
this area, and planted
jasmine, clematis
virginiana, and climbing
hydrangea along the
walls and railings.

Luxury at Any Age

PROSPECT PARK WEST

ABOVE Glass-bead wallpaper (made of round plastic beads of slightly varying sizes) gives the entry hallway sparkle and an immediate sense of luxury.

When Leyden Lewis transformed this two-bedroom apartment on Prospect Park into a haute-modern luxury pad, he did not do it for a young hip newcomer to the neighborhood. His client was a ninety-one-year-old woman, a "sage," as he refers to her, who has lived in Brooklyn for many years and originally emigrated from Israel. She wanted something practical—a stairless, barrier-free residence with easier access to the park and a view of the city—but was also amenable to playing with an open plan as well as unconventional materials. Lewis, whose Dumbo-based design studio combines architecture with interior design, had to put himself in the owner's shoes to meet her fundamental needs. At the same time, he was given free rein to create something special, cutting-edge, and resplendent with sumptuous surfaces.

The apartment had been previously divided into smaller, more conventional rooms and narrower passageways, and so Lewis masterminded a floor plan that flows around a "donut of circulation" so that the owner would never have to backtrack in order to move forward. The spacious entry hallway, which Lewis gave extra depth, offers easy passage into the four main areas of the residence—dining room and kitchen, master suite, guest quarters, and living room—all of which have open plans and pocket doors to make them truly barrier-free.

While visualizing the interior design elements, Lewis thought of the places his client would have visited in Europe in the early twentieth century, and how beautifully decorated they would have been. He was inspired by Art Nouveau and the Vienna Secession to bring sinuous lines and bronze accents into the design. "Certain areas in the apartment are reinforced by curves and flow more easily because of them," he explains. Details such as sandblasted stainless-steel bathroom rails were thought of not as add-ons but as integral parts of the design as a whole. "Instead of adding them to the bathroom as appendages, the room was created around the fluidity of their lines," says Lewis.

Both he and the owner share immigrant backgrounds (Lewis's family is from Trinidad and Tobago), and they would talk about how Brooklyn has helped their communities to remain vibrant. Says Lewis, "Brooklyn still feels like it is flourishing from the time when immigrant populations were first thriving here." More than a progressive designer making an of-the-moment home for a client, this project was also about a meeting of the minds—of two generations and of two dedicated Brooklynites.

The extra-deep entry hall acts as a central interior "courtyard" from which the other areas in the apartment open up. Standing in the dining room (which shimmers with purple Thai-silk walls by Jim Thompson/ Jerry Pair), one can see all the way into the living room through wide pocket doors that bring in light even when closed. The doors are made of bronze cladding over steel frames inset with Bendheim laminated textured glass, fabricated in collaboration with Face Design. The floor is untanned natural leather tiles from Edelman leather. The pendant light is by Fontana Arte (c. 1966).

OPPOSITE AND ABOVE
The lush surfaces in the
living room, such as the
Carini Lang silk custom
carpet, called "Tree and
Cloud," Donghia Volume
sofa, and armchairs by
Veronesi of Milan (1955),
reiterate the soft curves
of the fireplace surround.
The walls and ceilings
throughout are coated
with diamond plaster, and
pocket doors balance
circulation with privacy.

RENOVATION / **PARK SLOPE**

LEFT The bathroom is completely customized, with handrails of sand-blasted stainless steel and curved cabinets that echo the overall design.

BELOW In the shower, Lewis designed a comfortable bench and floor made of reclaimed and harvested teak.

OPPOSITE The kitchen features a curved peninsula swirled underneath a custom Cyla chandelier by jGoodDesign. Leyton Lewis/Leyton Lewis Design Studio designed the outer cabinetry with bleached anigre wood veneer and solid maple interiors. The lower cabinets under the kitchen peninsula are lacquered with a hand-rubbed finish. All millwork in the kitchen was constructed by Shoichi Hamano. The cabinets above the stove have laminated textured inset glass by Bedheim and hand-blackened steel doorframes by Face Design.

RENOVATION / PARK SLOPE

Intact with a Twist

MIKE D'S TOWNHOUSE

ABOVE Most of the house's period detail, including the floral crown molding, was intact. Tamra Davis recreated pieces of the delicate molding out of clay to patch missing areas.

OPPOSITE Bug silhouettes decorate the Studio Job armoire in the parlor.

Mike Diamond, aka Mike D of the Beastie Boys, and Tamra Davis, a filmmaker, moved to Brooklyn primarily because their sons attend school in the borough. "We were coming from Lower Manhattan every morning, and our lives became more entwined with things Brooklyn," says Diamond. "There was also something alluring and quiet about it in comparison to our Lower Manhattan home."

The brick townhouse they settled on in Cobble Hill still had its original details—such as floral crown molding in the entry hall and wide-plank pine floors—and they envisioned shaping the rooms with unique pieces by new designers. By combining international creations with many found locally in Brooklyn, the couple fashioned a home that puts a fun twist on the traditional nineteenth-century townhouse interior.

"One of the things that we liked about the house was that it had intact period detail. But we, I think, are perennially adolescent, so even though I like the elegance of period detail, I like to juxtapose it with other fluid and current ideas and not have to be so referential," Diamond explains. The couple had owned mid-century modern furniture in their previous home in Manhattan, but Diamond wanted to move away from everything mid-century and bring in all-new pieces. His criterion was when you looked at the piece you could see that it was made by a specific artist.

Diamond and Davis were pleasantly surprised by the amount of compelling design they found in Brooklyn. Many of their light fixtures were designed and fabricated in nearby Red Hook, by Bec Brittain, whose piece they have in their kitchen, and by Pelle. Wallpaper by Shanan Campanaro of Eskayel, in Williamsburg, adorns a wall in Davis's office on the second floor. The curtains installed in the parlor, master bedroom, and downstairs screening room were custom-designed and made by Elodie Blanchard of ElasticCo, based in Gowanus.

They worked with interior designer Paula Rodriguez and architects John and Jill Bouratoglou, who reconfigured the top master floor and reorganized the third floor to include their sons' rooms with a playroom in between. They punched three louvered doors off the kitchen-dining room on the parlor level, opening onto the southern-facing deck. Finally, the garden floor was lightened up with louvered glass doors on the back and divided into a screening room, as well as Diamond's office and studio.

ABOVE The large white wooden armoire in the parlor, made by the Dutch design collective Studio Job, is a perfect example of the artist's presence in each piece. As one approaches, the graceful stenciled pattern of bug silhouettes comes into focus.

"I think for family living a townhouse is the ideal, because it really gives great definition to space," Diamond contends. "You'd be hard-pressed to program a loft or an apartment that well in terms of definition. There's a functionality in a townhouse that makes for a great family lifestyle."

The top three levels retain the wide-plank old-growth pine floors of the original house, which dates to the 1850s. Downstairs in the garden, where the floors were not in as good of shape, Diamond and Davis installed new pine that had been pickled to lighten the color. Likewise, for the ceiling of the main entry hall, Davis re-created missing pieces of the delicate floral crown molding out of clay. These processes, along with the other inventive decisions the couple made in decorating their home, pay tribute to the authentic structure of the house while at the same time bringing it playfully into the modern moment.

ABOVE Each piece in the parlor living room is unique, from the black coffee table designed by Martin Baas to the brightly patterned chairs by Patricia Urquiola. ElasticCo made the draperies, lightly decorated with grommet holes. The chandelier was designed by Diamond and interior designer Paula Rodriguez. In some cases, the couple purchased antique pieces and updated them. Davis found the couch in the parlor on eBay and had it stripped, painted black, and reupholstered in black Ultrasuede. The carpet is a Beni Oaurain from Morocco, 1970. Diamond and Davis found this and the master-bedroom rug at Breuckelen Berber in Red Hook.

ABOVE Rodriguez saw Art Deco-style shelves in a Paris flea market, inspiring this design for the dining room. The shelves were fabricated out of brass and glass by ESP Metal Crafts in Brooklyn. The dining table and chairs were handmade by Chris Lehrecke. A Blossom Chandelier by Tord Boonje hangs over the table.

OPPOSITE Davis had seen a combination of brass, marble, and wood at a restaurant in Los Angeles, and they designed the hanging kitchen shelves with this in mind. A local metalworks shop that makes bar rails fabricated the shelves out of brass, and Bec Brittain's SHY light fixture was installed to intertwine with them.

Diamond and Davis worked with Nathan Shellkopf of Southslope Woodworks to source reclaimed wood for the kitchen paneling and other areas, but they specifically did not want the wood to look reclaimed and sought a more refined quality. Shellkopf milled the wood and finished it to give it elegance while still gaining the environmental benefit of recycling materials.

ABOVE The exposed wood beams add contrast to the master bathroom, which incorporates black patterned wallpaper by Flavor Paper, as well as a Bubble Chandelier by Pelle.

LEFT Davis found the double mirror in the master bathroom on Craigslist and had it painted black to make it look contemporary.

ABOVE The dropped ceiling on the top floor was opened up to uncover old beams and a surprising height. Diamond and Davis made this the master suite. The curtain rods, hung with drapes by ElasticCo, were raised to accentuate the ceiling height. The bed is an antique, which they had stripped and refinished to appear more modern. Above the bed hangs a photograph by Richard Misrach.

LEFT Davis collaborated with the street artist Olek to create the crocheted chandelier. The hanging desk is an antique from India.

RIGHT Diamond and Davis's sons share a middle room for desks as well as toys. Davis came up with the hook-on shelving above the desk, and Diamond designed the shielded light fixture.

ABOVE AND LEFT For the garden level, Diamond designed a custom wallpaper, Brooklyn Toile, with his friend, designer Vincent J. Ficarra of Revolver New York. Diamond researched classic French toile to guide the overall formula for the pattern, swapping out the typical bucolic hunting scenes for Nathan's hot dogs floating in the clouds, a bust of the rapper Biggie Smalls, a graffiti-decked subway train, and images of the Cyclone and the Brooklyn Bridge. Ficarra hand-drew each element, and Flavor Paper printed the pattern.

RENOVATION / COBBLE HILL

Unexpected Vintage

BELLOCQ TEA ATELIER

ABOVE AND BELOW The exterior of Bellocq Tea Atelier in Greenpoint belies the refined spaces the owners have created inside.

OPPOSITE The owners added a fireplace to the tearoom to bring it closer to a turn-of-the-twentieth-century parlor than a warehouse space. The room is furnished with white wood pieces that Scott built and Michael upholstered in pale-rose velvet. The chandelier hanging in the center of the room is a salvaged piece.

After fashioning a successful pop-up tea shop on Kings Road in London, Heidi and Scott Stewart and Michael Shannon set out to establish a permanent location for their Bellocq Tea Atelier in Greenpoint, Brooklyn. All three of Bellocq's proprietors have extensive experience in building and styling beautiful interiors, and so were able to execute a full transformation of a 5,000-square-foot warehouse, carving out two elegant and inviting rooms for sampling and purchasing tea that appear as though they've been there for a century. This way, they can have both a vintage-feeling space conducive to teatime and a large hidden area in back for blending.

Scott brought in salvaged wood from Pennsylvania to give the floors a wide-planked, country feel. In the shop, the team created rich aubergine plaster walls, giving the space the cool quality of an old stone enclosure, completely unexpected when stepping in off the industrial street outside. The color also serves as the backdrop for Bellocq's signature tea caddies in sunflower yellow, a color they chose specifically to stand out against the purple wall color.

Scott carried the whitewashed look of the wood-beamed ceilings onto the brick walls of the tearoom. He installed a chimney and fireplace in the room and purposefully placed it to be seen from the front entrance, inviting customers in and to the left where they can peruse the tea caddies. He washed the chimney brick with paint as well to integrate it with the surrounding original brick walls.

The story behind the name Bellocq says a lot about the venture itself. E. J. Bellocq was an early twentieth-century photographer famous for his portraitlike photographs of prostitutes in New Orleans. It is the "communication of beauty in unexpected places" that Scott says he admires so much about Bellocq's work, and which inspired the creation of the tearoom. "People notice the hard work and effort we put into it," he admits.

Bellocq's owners
designed these tea
caddies and labels
to evoke a bygone
era when tea was
a main commodity.
The sunflower yellow
vibrates against the
aubergine walls. Long
planks of reclaimed
wood from Philadelphia
were installed for floors,
and wood salvaged from
upstate New York was
used to build the shop
counter and shelves.

An Artist-Repurposed Factory
THE INVISIBLE DOG ART CENTER

OPPOSITE The left side of the building remains a wide elevator shaft, large enough to hold carriages in the early days. One resident artist, Giuseppe Stampone, with the help of his father and his friend Davide Sottanelli, painted the interior of the shaft with the words of Dante's *Inferno*, which permanently wrap the brick walls from the first floor to the third in fourteenth-century script.

BELOW 51 Bergen Street in Boerum Hill was originally a carriage factory. A century later, it became famous for manufacturing the Invisible Dog novelty item.

Lucien Zayan came from Paris in 2008 to visit some Brooklyn friends and never left. "I 'met' this building through a friend who owned a gallery in the neighborhood," he confides. "The building inspired the project. Even five minutes before, I never thought about doing something like this." The abandoned factory building in question was built in 1863 on Bergen Street in what is now the heart of Boerum Hill. The owner at the time was selling the property with everything in it. Originally a carriage factory, the building also had a life as a belt manufacturer, which became famous in the 1960s for making the Invisible Dog novelty item. When Lucien bought it, he inherited thousands of belt buckles, as well as an unforgettable name for the arts center he dreamed of establishing.

Since its launch in 2009, the Invisible Dog Art Center has burgeoned into a self-sufficient artists' collaborative, offering inexpensive studio space to thirty-five artists, designers, metalworkers, dancers, and performing artists, as well as extended residencies. Lucien was involved in theater in his native France and so wanted to create a space where new theater, dance, and art could come to life without the usual monetary hurdles.

Inside, remnants of the building's past decorate the walls and hallways. The studios are havens of repurposing, where old desks and flat files find new life, abandoned stools and chairs become furniture once again, and light fixtures provide light as well as carry out the center's ultimate vintage aesthetic.

OPPOSITE AND LEFT
Each artist's studio is the result of taking an old factory building and appropriating it to its new cause.

BELOW Above the stage in the main space is the first artwork that Lucien commissioned for the center, created by brothers Steven and William Ladd for the opening: a chandelier that glows like an illuminated tapestry made of ten thousand belt buckles (left behind with the building) and attached, drapelike, from the ceiling.

A Little Tradition, a Little Rock 'n' Roll

LINCOLN PLACE

ABOVE Fitzhugh Karol of The Brooklyn Home Company shaped the cherry wood kitchen counter stools with a chain saw, sanded them, and gave them a whitewash stain. He also crafted the sapele mahogany countertop.

OPPOSITE Bill and Kembra Caleo painted their entryway black, showing preserved plaster detailing as well as woodwork in a new light. They used the Surrey color from Ralph Lauren.

Painting a wall black may seem counterintuitive when the quest is usually to bring light into a townhouse interior, but Bill and Kembra Caleo pull it off beautifully. In the entry hall, the original details of the wood banister and wainscoting, as well as the decorative plasterwork along the stair, pop just as much as they would if the wall behind them were painted white. The space feels like the nineteenth-century vestibule that it is, and yet it has been made utterly contemporary.

"The goal was to honor the past but give the details a fresh life by adding the unexpected paint color," says Bill. "A little tradition, a little rock 'n' roll. Our children rub their hands on the cake molding as they are carried up the stairs at night, and I imagine the children who lived in the home more than a hundred years before us did the same thing."

The theme of preserving and painting the Victorian details in the house continues in almost every room. Both the dining room and kitchen have been coated in pure white, which sets off the dark wood floors and custom carved-wood furniture. Bill Caleo established The Brooklyn Home Company (TBHCo), a design-and-build group based in Columbia Heights, and the team put their expertise to good use in his own home.

Upstairs, the sitting room between the master bedroom and bathroom again upsets the norm. Kembra uses one papered wall for an installation of her collection of Louboutin shoes, which hang their heels on simple stock crown molding. The unexpected color they provide, much like the painted-black entry hall below, turns a traditional room into a space that will be relevant for years to come.

Karol carved the dining-room table legs out of wax before casting them in bronze and setting a solid piece of cherry wood on top. The worked texture of the legs offers a pleasant place to rub one's feet. The dining chairs are Louis Ghost Chairs by Philippe Starck. In the kitchen, the white walls and white-painted moldings set off the red wax-dipped chandelier created by Karol.

Kembra Caleo has created an art installation out of her Louboutin shoes in the sitting room next to the master bedroom. The wall treatment is a simple off-white with a metallic color stripe. A black fur rug adds warmth and texture, as does the dark wood detailing.

Open House CLINTON STREET

ABOVE Originally, a wall in the corridor divided the hallway and staircase from the parlor rooms.

OPPOSITE BArC Studio created an open-plan kitchen, dining room, and living room.

Relocating to Brooklyn from San Francisco, Emma Webb and Roger Scott sought a family home for their two young sons that would also support their creative careers. Webb, who has her own branding design firm, wanted a home office. In the Carroll Gardens brownstone the couple renovated, family and career strike a balance. It's also where an old Brooklyn house meets a modern-day family's needs.

"Brooklyn was fresh to us. We were picking up on the hexagonal tile and cozy dark wood, and we wanted to pay homage to those old features of the house," says Webb. "At the same time, the formal structure of a townhouse is not conducive to the way we live."

The 1900 brownstone had been occupied by three generations of one family, and the previous owners had raised boys who used to slide down the banister. Webb and Scott wanted to capture some of this past life in the new design, and that was part of the impetus for keeping the banister original. However, the house had endured such structural damage that most of the interiors had to be stripped to the bone.

Webb immediately clicked with architects Catherine Clark and Clementina Ruggieri and interior designer Miranda Harris of Brooklyn Architectural Coop (BArC Studio), based in Williamsburg. As a trio, they work collaboratively on every project from start to finish.

Webb's initial design concept of creating flexible spaces throughout grew out of the need to maximize space and light in the narrow townhouse. BArC showed how they could remove the wall dividing the front and back parlor rooms as well as the wall separating the stairwell and insert a long beam in the ceiling for support, creating an open-plan living and dining floor that extends to the deck outside. The back wall was replaced with sliding glass doors.

The kitchen unit clearly distinguishes itself as an insertion into the framework of white walls and natural wood floors on the parlor level. Similarly, upstairs in the master bedroom, the space is open, with all three windows exposed. BArC envisioned the middle spaces on each floor as changeable, with sliding pocket doors. Webb's office door on the third floor closes for privacy, and then tucks away for an open connection to her children one flight down.

Each architectural element adds to the formality of the visual space, whereas the functionality of the open plan and natural white-oak floors give it warmth. "As a designer I need that formality," Webb explains. "But I also need the humanity of the stuff that gets laid on top of it, all the wood and the natural light."

ABOVE AND RIGHT
Coming from California,
Webb and Scott wanted
a sense of nature on
the parlor level, which
inspired the sliding glass
doors off the kitchen
as well as the exposed
wood-burning fireplace.
Webb loves the desert,
and so the pale wood
and white walls give a
sense of an outdoor space
that is arid and vast.

LEFT The architectural
elements have been
pared down to maximize
the space, while the
crisp black lines of
the heating and cooling
vents, the Black Absolute
granite bench that
extends from the fireplace,
and the black stair
banister and runner add
a sharp graphic quality.

Doug Newton created custom brass lighting pieces for the house, including these hanging pendants above the dining table.

Upstairs in the master bedroom, BArC introduced a partial wall with clear definition from the floor to create a long and narrow enclosure for the bathroom. Working with Webb, they conceived the space as empty and thus flexible, the oval-shaped freestanding bath, marble shower, toilet, and vanity treated like distinct sculptural elements.

ABOVE The architects marked where the bathtub would go in laying out the room.

RIGHT Since each part of the house reflects the light differently, the rooms, even when all white, show subtle variations in hue. BArC Studio innovated ways of bringing light as well as a sense of warmth into the home, especially during the winter months. On the top floor, a pane of yellow translucent glass introduces the sensation of sunlight.

RENOVATION / CARROLL GARDENS

LEFT AND BELOW LEFT
Miranda Harris of
BArC Studio designed
the shiny-and-matte-
black tile pattern in
this vestibule, and
masterminded mirroring
the black exterior door
with a white version,
which lets in light
through fogged glass.

ABOVE A blackboard
strip above the
mahogany Shaker
pegs designed by
Harris echoes the
kitchen backsplash.

ABOVE The vestibule had pink and black tile before renovation.

ARCHITECTS' VOICE:

C. CLARK, M. HARRIS, C. RUGGIERI

BArC STUDIO

Design is only as good as its concept. We always strive to have a strong concept behind what we're designing, because if you don't and it doesn't hold up in a conversation, then it won't hold up in reality.

What is important to us is the idea of always being able to see the perimeter of a space. In this house, our project was to peel back the layers to respect the physical, sculptural space and then remold it in certain areas, such as to create the fireplace. The kitchen is very much an insert; instead of building it in, it is clearly saying, "I'm not a part of the skin." Then there are the negative recesses into the insertions, painted black, that create this relationship with the black linear elements.

The idea behind Brooklyn Architectural Coop (BArC Studio) is to bring in local designers to collaborate on a project. Miranda is an interior designer who is part of the team, working on each and every project. She is a trained sculptor and has an appreciation for color and texture that adds so much to any architectural design. She participates in discussions about sculptural space just as much as Clementina and I do, and we think about texture and color just as much as she does. There is no distinction between the roles, which is really quite unique. The more projects we do, the more people we bring in, and the more Brooklyn Architectural Coop grows. It's organic and stimulates a creative community, gathering collaborators as we go.

Reclaiming the Country for the City

RUCOLA

ABOVE Repurposed cans serve as planters hung on the window grills that give Rucola its unique character.

BELOW The restaurant Rucola sits unassumingly on a residential corner in Boerum Hill; inside, the owner drew inspiration from an 1886 barn.

The interior of the corner restaurant Rucola, in the historic district of Boerum Hill, was inspired by a barn. There are certain hints of this, although more refined elements—such as a marble bar top, shiny dining chairs, and ornate black ironwork on the windows, not to mention the Northern Italian menu—also have their say.

Rucola's owner, Henry Moynahan Rich, had visited a friend at Shelburne Farms in Vermont, and they hosted a dinner party in the 150-foot-long breeding barn one night. "It was so magical, I wanted to re-create a similar environment for people to dine in," says Rich. "Rucola is a much smaller space and in a brownstone as opposed to the middle of a field, but we chose materials that had the same relaxed character of the country."

"Somewhere in between Victorian delicacy and rural agrarianism" was the directive Rich gave to Bill Hilgendorf of Uhuru Design in Red Hook and Nadja Bruder, who led the interior design. Hilgendorf collected stills from movies Rich sent to him as inspiration and extracted textures and details from various interior shots—distressed walls, dark woody tones, old brick and marble, as well as rusty metal and reclaimed wood—to make a mood board.

The designers wanted to take advantage of the low ceiling height and give the room warmth, and so built the ceiling out of an old pine fence that had come down in eastern Pennsylvania. Reclaimed barn wood from Virginia created a country floor. Hilgendorf explains, "We wanted the place to have a contemporary feel with the materials and finishes telling a story of their past, so in a way it felt like it had always been there."

Wooden crates stacked
against one column
reinforce the rustic feel.

ABOVE The ornate iron
window grills were intact
when Rich found the
space, and they work
in harmony with the
refined country interior.

Wrapping the ceiling in salvaged pine allowed for more interesting details around the soffits. The marble bar counter pops against the wood tones throughout.

Rucola

DRAFT BEERS
- gaffel kölsch 6 · six point 7
sweet action
· southern tier 7
IPA

COFFEE AND TEA
· coffee 1.92   · latte 4   iced coffee 3
· espresso 2.50   · macchiato 3 iced latte 3.50
· cappucino 3.15 · americano 2.50 · tea 3

earl grey, assam,
chamomile, mint
jasmine green

Past Lives Reassembled WASHINGTON AVENUE

ABOVE AND BELOW
The Graham Home for
Old Ladies retains its
original brick facade
and insignia. The interior
was given a modern
renovation and converted
into apartments.

Nadia Yaron and Ry Scruggs create furniture and fabrics from recycled or reclaimed materials, and when they conceive of a space from top to bottom—as they did for Anitha Gandhi's Clinton Hill apartment—the effect is bright, airy, and completely one of a kind. Since Gandhi is Indian and owns a number of Indian statues as well as artwork from Africa and Haiti, the interior design became a collaboration not only between designer and client, but also between rustic vintage and vibrant color. The overall look is consistent and yet each piece traveled from a different place, repurposed by Yaron and Scruggs in ways no one else could have visualized.

The remodeled two-bedroom that Gandhi had purchased conveyed nothing about the 1851 building in which it lived, originally a home for elderly women. Yaron and Scruggs, who operate the Williamsburg-based design studio Nightwood, source items on Etsy and eBay, as well as at the Brooklyn Flea, among other places, and what they find and put together generates a unique energy, one that intersects old furnishings with all-natural fabrics—hand-dyed, woven, or embroidered.

To give depth and a weathered look to the living room, Yaron and Scruggs brought in painter Fernando Emilio Lucas to execute the first few coats of faux-stucco green walls, then added a more detailed layer themselves. Exposing the brick column also aged the interior and balanced it with the Indian artifacts Gandhi inherited from her parents.

The shoe rack provides structure to the apartment entrance. Emilio Lucas, who painted the walls, also painted the black-and-white checkerboard floor in the kitchen.

ABOVE Nightwood chose the fabrics throughout for a mix of colors and textures and for their loose, casual, lived-in feel. On the dining bench, from left to right, the pillow fabrics vary from vintage brown stripes to linen. The dining window seat is burlap with leather draped over it.

Nightwood envisioned window treatments that weren't curtains or drapes but that still provided privacy. "We wanted something flexible, that could be opened and closed for light when needed. We also wanted to bring in an old-world element to complement the washed walls," explains Yaron. They designed wooden shutters, which add unexpected beauty to every room: poplar in the guestroom and living room and butternut in the master bedroom.

In a space that was done top-to-bottom by a design team, one would expect a single-note feel, but that doesn't happen in this apartment. As they do with all of their projects, Nightwood took an original approach to this interior and let the materials speak for themselves, past lives and all.

Nightwood designed the freestanding bookshelf and cabinet, which Scruggs, who taught herself how to build and repurpose furniture, constructed out of a mix of barnwood, pine, poplar, and cedar.

Yaron fashioned the
seat cushion for this
vintage metal bench,
found on eBay, along
with the pillows in
different fabrics.

BELOW Framing out a salvaged headboard and footboard, Scruggs built a platform and transformed the piece into a bed again. Yaron made the mattress and mattress pad as well, choosing a blue ticking stripe to add to the aesthetic. The long bolster pillow was made by designer D. Bryant Archie.

A Brooklyn Stay

THE WYTHE HOTEL

ABOVE Brooklyn artist Tom Fruin fashioned the enormous hotel sign, fitted vertically into the corner scoop. An edgy and colorful mix of collaged tin signs from Fruin's collection, the neon letters provide the still-industrial (though quickly changing) surroundings with a beacon that glows day and night.

These days, the existence of the Wythe Hotel feels like an essential, if not inevitable, part of Williamsburg's evolution into a hipster epicenter. But in 2007, when real-estate developer Jed Walentas and Manhattan restaurateur Peter Lawrence hatched the plan to establish an inn in Brooklyn, the building at 80 Wythe Avenue was troublingly far from the subway. They took the risk anyway, because the structure itself, a 1901 cooperage that became a fabrics factory in the 1940s, had the right amount of character—visitors from around the world would have a sense of Brooklyn's past and present when they stayed there, and this was the point.

"There wasn't a place in Brooklyn where you could rent a hotel room and still feel like you were in Brooklyn," says Lawrence. Their dream was to create an indigenous space, one that conveyed the neighborhood's industrial style. When Andrew Tarlow, who created the iconic Williamsburg dining establishments Diner and Marlow & Sons, among others, came on board to give the hotel a restaurant, the team was at last complete, and in 2012, the first truly "Brooklyn" hotel opened its doors.

The partners brought in architect Morris Adjmi to design the hotel. Their goal was to introduce industrial loft living—a fundamental aspect of Williamsburg's identity—to a hotel stay. Known for their sensitivity to old buildings, Adjmi's firm, MA, kept the building intact, including the scooped corner that once provided a shaft for barrels to be lowered down to the street. They preserved the tall arched window openings and constructed new ones to match the originals, and replaced the old glass with replica factory windows built for the twenty-first century. Beams and columns were preserved to retain the solidity of the building, and concrete floors were poured for the guest rooms in keeping with the Williamsburg loft feeling. At the same time, the floors were fitted with radiant heating to make them extra comfortable during colder months.

Into these loftlike hotel rooms, many of which have outstanding views of the Brooklyn waterfront and Manhattan through floor-to-ceiling windows, the partners—all of whom had a say in the design—inserted elements of pared-down luxury, calling upon local designers, craftsmen, and builders. With so much ground-up construction happening in Williamsburg in recent years, the Wythe Hotel stands by its roots, and even those elements fashioned today keep the past in mind.

One feat was to create a curved glass door for the hotel entrance, which would mimic the bend of the scoop. It took several tries, but the partners did succeed in locating a glass expert, a metalworker, and a mechanic to get the door swinging open a few thousand times a day. The brick walls throughout the hotel were carefully cleaned, but not so much as to erase all remnants of paint. The idea was to expose the brick while also maintaining the trace of the building's past.

ABOVE AND OPPOSITE
TOP Wallpaper created
for the hotel by designer
Dan Funderburgh and
printed at Flavor Paper
in Boerum Hill appears
in three patterns based
on old-fashioned toiles.
The designs speak to the
building's turn-of-the-
century history and fall
in line with the black
Thonet–inspired bent-
wood chairs; the

marble-topped coffee
tables, café tables, and
countertop; and the desks
custom made from the
salvaged roof timber.
All of the beds were
made by Dave Hollier,
whose woodshop is
around the corner.
Sawyer DeVuyst of
SAWFurniture designed
and fabricated the
pale-green side tables.

OPPOSITE LEFT
The terrace off of a
duplex suite has
breathtaking panoramic
views of the East River
and Manhattan, with
modern-day Adirondack
chairs and ottomans
to help guests take
them in.

OPPOSITE RIGHT
Elements of comfort
in the loft-like suite
include an over-dyed
oriental rug, a leather
couch, and marble-
topped kitchen counters
and coffee table.

Time Traveler REYNARD

OPPOSITE Reynard owner Andrew Tarlow hired Aleksey Kravchuk to design and fabricate all of the lighting in the restaurant, which refers back in time without imitating the period, featuring glass globes and brass armatures. Kravchuk also designed the steel-and-glass archways at the entrance to the restaurant, incorporating fogged window glass salvaged from the original factory.

BELOW Tarlow designed the bar and commissioned his friend Kevin McKeown to execute it, integrating a large vintage mirror and marble countertop. The tile floor was designed by Tarlow and installed by the Taggios Brothers.

As both a longtime Williamsburg restaurateur and partner in the Wythe Hotel, Andrew Tarlow was free to do whatever he wanted when it came to designing the hotel restaurant, Reynard. Named for the fabled miscreant fox with a heart, the dining establishment mixes turn-of-the-century elegance with the daily beat of travel, balancing the atmospheres of a café, bar, and high-end dining room in one lofty space.

"I thought of it as grand, with high ceilings," Tarlow explains. "I wondered how it could happen inside this building, how it could become a gathering space for tourists who are visiting as well as people who live here. And how do all of those groups come together in a singular, grand room? I thought of European train stations and all those gathering spaces of the early twentieth century."

Tarlow worked with the same team of craftsmen that had built his other restaurants to take advantage of the ground floor's full height. He brought in Aleksey Kravchuk of Works Manufacturing to create lighting pieces that hang from the high ceilings, humanizing them while keeping them lofty. The arched detailing in the back dining room, combined with the exposed steel columns, banquettes, and multiplicity of windowpanes, evokes European termini such as the Gare du Nord in Paris. At the same time, the tiled floor in the front café area pays tribute to old-time New York, as does the intricately carved bar. Within a 1901 building that has been converted into an up-to-the-minute hotel, nothing feels more appropriate than a restaurant that harkens back to meeting points of the past.

"There will come a time here in Brooklyn and all over America, when nothing will be of more interest than authentic reminiscences of the past," foretold the late nineteenth-century poet and *Brooklyn Daily Eagle* editor Walt Whitman in 1861.[1] The importance of restoring and preserving Brooklyn's history, in the form of a parlor door, a brownstone, a park, or a neighborhood, has become more apparent than ever at a time of rapid residential and commercial development. Meeting this need is a growing interest in original objects and structures in Brooklyn. The lengths to which a homeowner will go to bring a row house back to 1881 or the years a community group will invest to restore a park monument for its centennial indicate just how critical it is that these restorations happen now.

At Jane's Carousel in Brooklyn Bridge Park, years of careful restoration meet the work of an internationally renowned architect, simultaneously preserving an old object and giving it a second life. Treasure troves like Eddie's Salvage Shop in Clinton Hill tell the story of Brooklyn home restoration through the items they take in, clean up, and put on display. A Victorian brownstone in Bedford-Stuyvesant can come full circle through the attentive preservations conducted by its owner and local artisans. In Prospect Park South, a stand-alone family home guides its new owners in restoring it whole, helping to resurrect a unique neighborhood in the heart of the borough. Again and again, Brooklyn residents tell how their old houses steered them in keeping what was important and authentic.

1. Walt Whitman, *The Uncollected Poetry and Prose of Walt Whitman*, edited by Emory Holloway (Garden City, NY: Page & Co., 1921).

2

RESTORATION

Victorian Brownstone in Bloom HANCOCK STREET

ABOVE Daniel Thompson's 1881 Bedford-Stuyvesant brownstone, designed by Isaac Reynolds, is situated on a block of row houses developed around the same time.

OPPOSITE Thompson hired the Tamer brothers in Boerum Hill to restore and hang these parlor doors. They worked on them for about a month and put in Dutchman patching to repair any holes. It took them a day to balance and hang them in place.

Growing up in a Victorian house in Kansas City, Daniel Thompson was enthralled with the period at an early age, and began collecting Victorian furniture when he was as young as sixteen. When he set out to find a home in Brooklyn, he fell in love with the row houses in Bedford-Stuyvesant and purchased one in 2000. He worked to restore it over the next several years, bringing it back to the original dwelling of 1881 as closely as he could.

When Thompson bought the brownstone, the state of the interior was somewhat of a time capsule. It had not been lived in, except on one floor, for many years. The cellar was filled with old mattresses and furniture. The whole place was dusty, and many of the floors were covered in linoleum and carpeting. Most of the woodwork was painted, and on the parlor level it had been given a coat of varnish that had darkened over time. Thompson did some tests on the wood and discovered that it was American black walnut, harvested from old-growth North American forests, which have since become extinct.

Thompson hired Arthur Wala, who had trained in Poland as a carpenter in historical preservation, and he got to work removing the old stain on the parlor and garden levels. Thompson was thrilled to find that much of the wood was burled, creating a beautiful natural patterning on the wainscoting throughout. He found the nine-foot-tall parlor doors only a few blocks away on Halsey Street, at a house that was being gutted. The doors fit the opening in his home perfectly. With further investigation he learned that the two houses shared the same architect, Isaac Reynolds. A prolific 1880s designer of brownstones in what was then Bedford, Reynolds worked primarily with the developer S.E.C. Russell.

"The Russell/Reynolds combination built a lot of these houses and so they probably sourced the same woodworkers," explains Thompson. "The doors even matched the moldings. You can find things locally because more likely than not they are from the same source." With some research, Thompson was able to uncover a good deal about the house's history and the earliest family known to have lived in it. John Nugent moved in with his family in 1895. The home had been plumbed for central heating as well as gas lighting all the way up to the top floor, indicating not only that it had been built for well-to-do occupants but also that it was the pinnacle of modern house design in its day.

ABOVE LEFT AND RIGHT
Original to the house,
the Gilbert locks in rose
bronze add a "mod-
ern" touch to the parlor
doors, as the decora-
tion on them links to the
Aesthetic movement of
the 1870s and '80s.

"Let's go down to dinner" was a common saying in the 1880s because the dining room rested on the garden level then, next to the butler's pantry and kitchen. Elaborate plasterwork depicting fruit and mahogany wainscoting make up the more ornate details found in the room, a formerly public area which Thompson has turned into his master bedroom.

In the backyard, Thompson re-created a moon garden, a particularly Victorian concept of planting a green space with nothing but white flowers. At twilight, the blooms glow and become more fragrant. "I like the historical quality and then I like the physical sense of a quiet, cool garden," says Thompson. He placed a mirror at the far end, another Victorian technique, to create the sense of continuous space. "Victorians tended to place mirrors throughout their houses as well, at the front door, at the end of hallways, and at the top of stairs to maximize the light from windows as well as candlelight as you walked up," Thompson explains.

The British craftsman and poet William Morris once instructed: "Have nothing in your home that you do not know to be useful, or believe to be beautiful." Thompson likes this quote. "Victorians believed that beautiful surroundings lifted the spirits," he says. "I find this to be utterly true."

Thompson has repurposed period
dresser mirrors for over the mantelpieces in the front and back parlors.

ABOVE Because
Thompson has been
collecting Victorian
furniture since he was
a teenager, he has
placed antique pieces
throughout his parlor
rooms, as well as
collections of Victorian
porcelain.

OPPOSITE The fireplaces were all intact when Thompson purchased the house, and in the front parlor and dining rooms, the surround is carved from rich chocolate marble, incised with linear decoration that in some places still shows its gold leaf. This was a technique of the Aesthetic movement, when a keen interest in Japanese art took hold and decoration became more stylized and abstract rather than realistic.

ABOVE Thompson's collection of porcelain Royal Worcester zoomorphic pieces, with animal-formed handles, dates from the 1880s.

ABOVE The silverplate tea service, made by Wm. Rogers Co. in Hartford, Connecticut, has an Anglo-Japanese pattern dating from the 1870s. The crystal glassware is T.G. Hawkes, from Corning, New York. The bowl is Val St. Lambert crystal.

Thompson displays white porcelain on his kitchen shelves.

ABOVE Carpenter Arthur Wala built the kitchen, which sits in its original location on the garden floor. Thompson drew up the designs and Wala created each piece to blend with the Victorian woodwork in the house. In the 1880s, the kitchen would have contained an iron cookstove and a freestanding farm table in the middle of the room. Thompson designed an island counter that looks like a table, which Wala gave turned legs, a cherry wood top, and a bead board surround that matches the wainscoting. All modern-day appliances are tucked out of sight. Refrigerated drawers pull out from under the counter. The drawer and cabinet pulls were salvaged and then sandblasted and replated by local craftsmen.

A very Victorian concept, Thompson's moon garden is meant to be a serene respite from the city in the evening. The lilies, moon vine, and nicotiana become more fragrant at night.

EDDIE HIBBERT

EDDIE'S SALVAGE SHOP

I opened up thirty years ago, but in different locales. I did a lot of flea markets and then set up this shop in '99. I always worked construction and demolition, and all of this stuff we were throwing out, people would actually run up to us and offer money for it. So I said, Wait a minute, there's something to be had with this. And what it came down to is they don't make this stuff anymore.

The appreciation level has really increased in the neighborhood, but it's always been here. This, along with people salvaging, the green movement, repurposing— this all goes hand in hand. A lady just bought a door, and she's going to make a dining-room table out of it. Another took a French door and made a chandelier out of it. She put four chains on the corners of the door, and she's got candles on each pane so when you light it the panes reflect. We call her the Canadian Martha Stewart.

I take anything architectural, because for the most part, even with a molding that's in relatively good condition, it's hard to find. Plus, that period style, that detail, is hard to find and match. When you go to Home Depot, they have what you call a finger joining in their moldings. It's not a solid piece, whereas the molding I have is one solid piece.

LEFT Eddie's Salvage Shop, on Greene Avenue in Clinton Hill, is a mecca of townhouse restoration and renovation. Eddie Hibbert, who used to work in construction, takes architectural remnants from houses that are demolished throughout the borough, so that new owners can find a home for them.

RIGHT Fireplace surrounds and mantels abound at Eddie's, as do doors taken out of Victorian and early nineteenth-century homes by developers and home renovators.

LEFT A door detail can be repaired and the whole used again.

BELOW The shop provides a number of services, including fixing furniture and stripping paint from century-old wood.

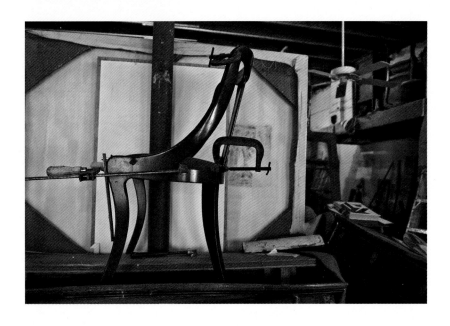

Gracious Authenticity ALBEMARLE ROAD

ABOVE This 1905 home in Prospect Park South was originally designed by the imaginative architect John Petit.

OPPOSITE The bend in the oak stair banister, shaped by a century of hands traveling up and down, has been retained for posterity's sake.

Chris and David Lindsay-Abaire (the Pulitzer Prize-winning playwright) called upon their friend Patricia Kelley of Kelley/Hemmerly Architecture and Design to lead the restoration of their 1905 freestanding house in Prospect Park South. As their goal was to bring in modern amenities without sacrificing the spirit and integrity of the original architecture, they had to make sure their collaborating architect respected their needs, and those of the house.

One of the many eclectic homes designed by the architect John Petit, the house, in terms of style, is utterly unique. Petit—whose firm Kirby, Petit & Green is known for the design of Dreamland, the Coney Island amusement park that burned down in 1911—masterminded many of the homes in the Prospect Park South development. The area in 1899 was Flatbush's newest "high-class residence district," realized by developer Dean Alvord. The aim was "to create a rural park within the limitations of the conventional city block and city street," as Alvord put it.[2] Grassy medians divide the broad streets in the community: one is off the grid and connected to it at the same time.

The Lindsay-Abaires' house still had many original elements when they purchased it; however, a doctor who had lived and worked there from 1959 to 1995 had reconfigured much of it to accommodate his office, patient rooms, and waiting room. Kelley proposed stripping away all that had been added or changed by the doctor to uncover the layout of the first residence. They gutted the office and exam rooms and removed the extension he had attached.

"What we found in the house influenced our renovation decisions," says Mrs. Lindsay-Abaire. "It became clear that so many of the 'improvements' to it had been made in the service of convenience, providing a quick and inexpensive solution to a problem. We wanted to remedy this Band-Aid approach to home design and repair wherever possible. When we needed to bring in brand-new elements, our aim was to make sure they married well with what was original to the house."

The result preserves a unique home dreamed up by one of Brooklyn's early freethinking architects. Modern accoutrements such as central air have been added, and yet the whisper hole on a top floor has been left in its place. The house is a perfect example of the old returning to be just as functional in the present while the new seamlessly hums behind it, out of view.

2. Francis Morrone, "John Petit's Visionary Home Designs," *New York Sun*, October 20, 2006.

ABOVE The stained-glass windows flanking the entry hall fireplace have remained intact since the house was built.

OPPOSITE TOP Features such as the columns, moldings, floors, tapestries, and many of the light fixtures all have stayed with the house since its conception and were given an accurate restoration by the architect and owners. The original oak paneling in the entry hall and along the stairs, including the oak railing, have been lovingly restored.

ABOVE New windows were designed to match the originals throughout, complete with the weight and chain lift system.

RIGHT This whisper hole on the third floor of the home once allowed residents to communicate with the kitchen.

OPPOSITE A restored gramophone sits in what once was the home's music room.

ABOVE The hardware, wall sconces, and hanging chandelier in the dining room are original. The intricately carved wood is mahogany and includes mantel and column decoration, door trims, and a built-in sideboard.

OPPOSITE TOP The oval-shaped mahogany dining room had been converted into a patient waiting area by the previous owner, with an entrance through the solarium attached to the room. Kelley and the owners restored the solarium's original structure, bringing in a replica leaded glass decorative window like the one that would have been in place in 1905.

OPPOSITE BOTTOM The built-in mahogany sideboard follows the curve of the oval dining room. The wall tapestries are original to the room.

A Monumental Ode to Brooklyn FORT GREENE PARK

ABOVE AND OPPOSITE
The McKim, Mead, and
White design for the
Prison Ship Martyrs'
Monument, finished
in 1908, called for a
neoclassical look, with
white granite steps,
a 150-foot Doric column
with a bronze lantern
cap, and a new
entrance to the tomb
of the prison ship martyrs.

Fort Greene Park is Brooklyn's first park. It was originally a public pasture and recreation area, and then became Fort Putnam during the American Revolution, supervised by American major general Nathanael Greene in 1776. It was surrendered to the British during the Battle of Long Island. The British held thousands of American captives on ships anchored in the East River, 11,500 of whom died of abuse, starvation, and disease, and their bodies were hastily buried along the shore. In 1808, the prisoners' remains were moved to a tomb near what is now Vinegar Hill.

In 1812, the fort on the hill was renamed Fort Greene for the Revolutionary War general and repurposed for the War of 1812. Once the threat passed, locals started to use the grounds for recreation again. In 1847, at the urging of poet Walt Whitman, then editor of the *Brooklyn Daily Eagle*, the city of Brooklyn designated the site as a park. Washington Park, as it was first named, was completed in 1850 to the design of Andrew Jackson Downing.

In 1867 landscape architects Frederick Law Olmsted and Calvert Vaux, who had designed some of America's most iconic parks—such as Yellowstone National Park, Manhattan's Central Park, and Prospect Park in Brooklyn—proposed a new layout for Washington Park and a design for a crypt to hold the remains of the "prison ship martyrs," as Whitman had named them. In the design, a trellised walk led to two flights of stairs descending to a circular parade ground in the northwest corner of the park. Olmsted and Vaux's layout and crypt were finished in 1873, and the remains were moved to their new resting place. In 1897, as part of Brooklyn's consolidation into greater New York City, the park was renamed Fort Greene Park to distinguish it from Washington Square Park in Manhattan.

As the result of an intense competition, the venerable architecture firm of McKim, Mead, and White was hired in 1905 to design a permanent monument to the prison ship martyrs. They created a new entrance to the crypt and wide granite stairs leading up to a plaza marked off by four granite posts, each one flanked by a magnificent bronze eagle. Stanford White designed the freestanding 150-foot granite Doric column with a bronze lantern as its crown (it was his last design before his murder in 1906). The monument was dedicated by president-elect William Howard Taft in 1908.

OPPOSITE The 1908 design included a plaza around the Prison Ship Martyrs' Monument, which underwent a thorough restoration in 2008.

BELOW The cast-bronze eagles were created by sculptor Adolph Alexander Weinman and installed at each granite corner post of the McKim, Mead, and White plaza. Replicas made from an early twentieth-century casting were installed in the park as part of its restoration.

In the 1930s another series of renovations were carried out by Parks Deparment architect Gilmore D. Clarke. In subsequent years, the bronze eagles were removed for restoration and placed in the New York City Parks Department headquarters in Manhattan. The plaque that had originally been the cornerstone of the Vinegar Hill crypt was removed and placed in storage, due to vandalism.

Beginning in 1997, what started as the garden committee under the Fort Greene Association and became the Fort Greene Park Conservancy worked to achieve a thorough restoration of the Prison Ship Martyrs' Monument and plaza. As Ruth Learnard Goldstein, the founding chair of the Fort Greene Park Conservancy, explains, "Nothing is static. There had been so many renovations of the park since 1908. We had to determine what was most authentic." They conducted research into how the plaza had been laid out and brought it back as closely as possible to the McKim, Mead, and White design.

The restoration of the Prison Ship Martyrs' Monument, including all four eagles and the plaque, was completed in 2008, on the centennial date of the McKim, Mead, and White dedication.

Home Keeper STERLING PLACE

ABOVE The entry hall in this Prospect Heights house has been pared down to the original wood.

OPPOSITE After stripping the stairs of several layers of paint, the floral newel post gleams in its natural element.

"Manhattan has lost a lot of its interest for me," says Prospect Heights dweller Laura Ljungkvist. She and her husband, Paul, bought their 1899 townhouse in 2004 and lived in it throughout the renovation process. The garden apartment had to be vacated and then remodeled so that they could make it their home while the upper three floors were completely gutted and rebuilt.

A children's book author, illustrator, and graphic artist, Ljungkvist explains, "The 'dirt in the corners' and the diversity that I found so charming when I moved to Manhattan in 1993 is not there anymore. Brooklyn is where everything is happening now."

When Ljungkvist and her husband purchased the house, it was divided into many tiny rooms. They took all of the walls down on the parlor level. Now, from the entrance hall, one walks into a spacious parlor, which is open to the dining area and kitchen in the back. The house is seventeen feet wide, yet it has a central staircase that lets the front and back parlor rooms on the first floor take full advantage of the width of the building, space an ordinary row house would not have.

They stripped several layers of white and turquoise paint from all of the woodwork in the house. Six men scrubbed with toothbrushes for almost three weeks to reach the original wood, and the result is breathtaking. The paint had helped to preserve superbly carved details around the entryway mirror, the parlor fireplace, and on the staircase newel posts and banisters. Ljungkvist and her husband had the walls painted white for contrast, and the effect is refreshingly modern and old-fashioned at once. In these open spaces, the couple placed selected mid-century modern pieces to create a sitting area by the carved-wood fireplace and a dining room.

Ljungkvist says she would never completely alter an old house to meet her own aesthetic ideal. She found many mementos from the past while renovating—layers of linoleum, carpet, old cigarettes, lipsticks, a page from a 1927 calendar—so that the house's history made itself known.

"It reminds you of all the people who have lived here and [its] history. Now this street is landmarked, so we can't really do whatever we want to the house anymore. But I think you can't anyway, because you don't really own a house like this; you're just a keeper of it for a little while."

ABOVE The stairs, now au naturel, pair beautifully with crisp white walls and one essential twenty-first-century element: a wall-hung bike.

RIGHT The tone of the original wood infiltrates the aesthetic throughout the house. "I am happy how we have been able to blend the modern in with the traditional," Ljungkvist says, referring to the black Papa Bear chair and brown-and-white cowhide rug in the sitting room.

ABOVE Upstairs in the family living room, modern Danish pieces sit comfortably among the abundant warm wood and white walls.

LEFT Ljungkvist found a number of relics during renovation, such as a 1927 calendar page and remnants of the original wallpaper and linoleum.

RESTORATION / PROSPECT HEIGHTS

Classic/ Contemporary WILLOW STREET

ABOVE Architect William B. Tubby remodeled the Federalist-style structure in the mid 1880s, replacing the square roofline and dormer windows with an Eclectic-Flemish facade—a Tubby trait. Joseph Vance Architects designed a new entry door in the style of Tubby, which changed the original solid door to one that is half glass to bring light into the parlor level.

The owners of this Brooklyn Heights home were not new to renovation when they purchased it in 2007. Having revived two houses before this one, the couple had a feel for the dual processes of restoration and remodeling. But there was major work to be done. The building had been divided into multiple apartments and called for a gut renovation to convert it to a single-family dwelling. There was so little light in the interior, the couple had second thoughts about buying it, but instead they seized the opportunity to put their expertise to the test.

Built circa 1831 in the Federalist style typical of the day, the house was redesigned in the late 1880s by renowned architect William B. Tubby, the creator behind many late nineteenth-century homes and public buildings in the area. Often with such old houses the question becomes, Which direction do you take: traditional or modern? The owners did something quite radical and took both, hiring Williamsburg-based Joseph Vance Architects, who pair a modern sensibility with an expertise in restoration, and interior designer Janet Liles, who is based in Boerum Hill.

The owners' two main directives were to bring in light and to create a home that combines but does not blend the modern and the traditional. Specifically, they wanted a modern ground floor and a similarly modern top floor, with the middle floors, which would contain the classic parlor, dining, and music rooms, restored to their original feel.

The garden level had no original detail to preserve, and here Vance designed a modernist space, with a comfortable media room in front, a cook's kitchen in the middle, and a family dining room divided from the outdoor patio by two walls of sliding glass doors. The backyard was dug out so that the dining room and garden could exist on the same level.

Upstairs, the story changed. The rooms did have original details to preserve, beautiful decorations from Tubby's day. But due to extensive damage over the years they had to be reconstructed. Such major restoration, however, did provide the opportunity to balance the two aesthetic extremes more effectively.

"As you ascend from the parlor up to the master floor and then to the kids' floor," Vance explains, "the door trims become more modern, and the traditional moldings start to lighten up."

In a neighborhood of some of the oldest residential structures in Brooklyn, this home pays homage to both the past and the present moment.

Tubby mirrored the facade with a distinctive fifty-foot brick chimney on the back of the building, supported by flying buttresses. The renovation of the house included a complete brick-by-brick reconstruction of the chimney.

LEFT Sleek walnut panels in the modern garden level meet the parlor floor's more classic aesthetic, where a new elevator stands across from a restored stair banister, made with the same walnut as the paneling. Vance and interior designer Janet Liles worked to tie the traditional elements to the modern ones through materials as well as paint colors.

RIGHT Joseph Vance Architects gave a nod to traditional wall paneling underneath the stairs.

ABOVE "The kitchen needed a little spark," says Liles. She and the owners came upon Smoldering Red by Benjamin Moore, and Liles added the Cherner barstools in Stella Orange wood finish to match.

RIGHT Liles brought the slate of the patio inside by giving the walls a gray palette. Moon River Chattel in Williamsburg custom built the dining table, which is oak with an iron base. Brooklyn-based Wonk made the walnut and graphite sideboard.

ABOVE LEFT AND RIGHT Vance's team researched molding profiles, wainscoting, and floor patterns from Tubby's day, and much of the window trim in the parlor remained for them to replicate. A painter who specializes in restorations, Phoebe M. Tremalio-Slater, was hired to re-create the coffered ceiling detail in the parlor. The black and gold table lamp was designed by Hippolyte Heizler, a mid-nineteenth-century French animal sculptor. Liles, who inventoried the owners' art and furniture collections before designing, brought in materials and made certain placements with these in mind. The fabric for the parlor draperies and the wallpaper in the vestibule set the tone for the floor.

OPPOSITE The formal dining room on the parlor level reveals a fresh take on a classic space, re-creating the inside of a Chinese lacquer box. Liles hired Tamer Restoration and Refinishing in Boerum Hill to extend the table to fit the room, and had the dining and side chairs reupholstered. The English Victorian polished brass chandelier designed by Christopher Dresser and the eighteenth-century Japanese screen are both from the owners' collection.

INTERIOR DESIGNER'S VOICE:

JANET LILES

JANET LILES INTERIOR DESIGN

Usually, an image just comes to me; it's not linear. A color, a form. A lot of designers have their stamp, but I'm not that way at all. I'm much more interested in channeling what clients want and then directing it. I like working with families and residential design because you get inside people's heads. With these owners, they had such a high level of aesthetic and were so experienced; they had such a respect and appreciation for the process.

The minute I saw the dining room, I said, "You have to have a red-lacquer room." And they said, "What?" We went back and forth and back and forth. My mother was born in China, and my first degree was in East Asian studies and Asian art history. And so when I told Phoebe (the ceiling painter) that I wanted a red-lacquer room, like a lacquer box, she said she had one and brought it one day. For me, the design process is like taking steps. Further along, things come together.

I had this vision for that room, like a movie set. I wanted you to sit at the table with a fine Bordeaux and truffles, the most extraordinary dark chocolate truffles, and a few raspberries. That would be the experience.

RIGHT AND OPPOSITE The Venetian Parchment wall covering in the dining room is by Jacobsen & Balla. Liles had the side chairs reupholstered in a Stroheim fabric called Paris.

Vintage Meets Nouvel

JANE'S CAROUSEL

ABOVE For the 1922 carousel she restored, Jane Walentas was advised to "dip and strip" the horses using a toxic chemical bath, repainting them with car enamels, which last longer but leave the horses looking spray-painted. "I thought our carousel was too important and elegant for this kind of treatment," she says.

OPPOSITE The contemporary French architect Jean Nouvel designed a seventy-two-foot-square year-round enclosure of steel and acrylic to house Jane's Carousel in Brooklyn Bridge Park.

The idea to place a classic carousel on the banks of the East River in Dumbo was born in the 1980s, when developer David Walentas was asked by the city to plan a state-owned waterfront park. Architect Ben Thompson introduced the carousel concept, but it would take many years and a number of iterations for the park, now called Brooklyn Bridge Park, to come to life. When Jane's Carousel opened in 2011, a 1922 work of restoration had found a new home—inside a stunning modern structure designed by the internationally renowned architect Jean Nouvel.

"Designing a building in one of the most beautiful sites in the city—between the Brooklyn Bridge and the Manhattan Bridge, facing Manhattan—was a challenge in itself," states Ateliers Jean Nouvel. "At the same time, Jane's Carousel is one of the loveliest historic carousels in America. Our architecture had to protect it while revealing and enhancing it."

The contrast of the two structures, one inside the other, serves to accentuate the individual, distinctive beauties of each. The carousel, built by the Philadelphia Toboggan Company in 1922, was in rare good condition when David's wife, Jane Walentas, found it in Idora Park in Youngstown, Ohio. But it had sixty years of park paint on it and needed to be restored. Walentas, an artist trained in graphic design and printmaking, used X-Acto blades, preserving the original paint layer with a shellac barrier, and then made plans to repaint it as close to the original colors as possible. The process required more than twenty years of research, scraping, and careful documentation with drawings, photos, and precise color matches.

From the beginning, Jane Walentas wanted a modern design for the shelter that would house the carousel. She says, "The site called for a sophisticated structure rather than a stereotypical reproduction. It was important for the carousel to be taken out of the realm of an ordinary amusement park ride." David Walentas had brought Jean Nouvel on board during a second planning phase for Brooklyn Bridge Park.

What Ateliers Jean Nouvel proposed was at first quite radical: a transparent acrylic cube rather than the cylindrical shape one might immediately imagine. As its purpose was to be a protective shelter and not to overshadow the carousel, the architects related the structure to the architecture of warehouses and industrial buildings so prevalent in Brooklyn. An ode to Brooklyn's industrial waterfront, the building Ateliers Jean Nouvel innovated evokes the right metaphor for both the carousel and the site itself: a jewel held delicately in its elegant box, a meeting point of the old and the new.

Above the carousel hangs a skylight equal in diameter. Made up of insulated glass units, it is supported by a cable-and-steel system inspired by the pole-and-cable structure of the carousel.

OPPOSITE The ceiling is made of polished aluminum strips separated by three-inch voids. The aluminum reflects the carousel's vibrant colors and lights to increase its presence, while the striping creates visual contrast.

LEFT This carriage detail shows the intricate restoration work led by Jane Walentas. During the last two years of restoration, Walentas hired a team of six artists in Dumbo to help finish the project. "We all painted, sanded, stenciled, varnished, applied gold and platinum leaf, and did whatever it took to restore the carousel to its original elegance," Walentas recalls.

ABOVE Ateliers Jean Nouvel employed a construction technique normally used in large aquariums to fix the acrylic panels on two sides to provide complete transparency. At the same time, the depth of the acrylic panels, four and a half inches thick, gives subtle distortions, so the city appears to dance through the material. The other two sides fold open from the center, echoing the folding doors on airplane hangars, reinforcing the character of a simple, square, industrial building.

There will always be innovations, but the particular ideas cultivated in Brooklyn architecture and design today will likely define what *innovative* means worldwide for decades to come. Selldorf Architects masterminds one of the first sustainable recycling centers built from recycled materials on the Sunset Park waterfront. H3 Hardy Collaboration Architecture transforms a Salvation Army building into a state-of-the-art performance space for the Brooklyn Academy of Music. Landscape designers bring their creations to the next level, embracing environmental measures of recycling rainwater and staunching overflow. At the Brooklyn Botanic Garden Visitor Center, architects WEISS/MANFREDI create a testing ground for growing better green roofs in urban environments, providing a model for city greenspaces around the world.

With a true gift for the ad hoc, Brooklyn designers are breaking the rules and building startlingly fresh structures and interiors out of unconventional materials. In a Prospect Heights townhouse, concrete parging becomes the perfect dining-room wall, and at the Bushwick restaurant Roberta's, the architectural elements and the interior furnishings are built from materials found on-site, running against the grain of formal interior decoration.

As Brooklyn becomes an increasingly international borough, the international design world will look to it for inspiration.

3

INNOVATION

Truly Ad Hoc ROBERTA'S

ABOVE A concrete
wall acts like wallpaper
in the extension.

BELOW Roberta's main
dining room was
created with whatever
elements were on hand:
doors for the family-
style tabletops,
mismatched light
fixtures, cinderblock
walls given a coat of
paint, and a pizza oven
installed by cutting a
hole in the roof.

OPPOSITE Parachini,
Hoy, and Mirarchi
had this pizza oven
shipped from the
Piedmont region
of Italy.

At Roberta's in Bushwick, what began as an emptied-out garage
has become a restaurant with aesthetic integrity because it
was created ad hoc. Owners Chris Parachini and Brendan Hoy
and chef Carlo Mirarchi started out simply, with a pizza oven
shipped all the way from the Piedmont region of Italy. They
installed the oven in the front of the building and fashioned
a chimney to fit. Inside the cinderblock walls of the main
dining space, they served pizzas, salads, and cured meats on
family-style tabletops made out of salvaged doors, to which
their in-house builder added custom-built legs and benches.

Outside, open to the elements, two shipping containers
that had been joined at an L were insulated to house the
recording studio for Heritage Foods Network, the online radio
arm of Heritage Foods USA, established by Patrick Martins.
The owners wanted to install a larger garden and greenhouse
on the roofs of the shipping containers. One night, California
restaurateur and chef Alice Waters dined at the restaurant and
enjoyed it so much she pitched in so the dream could be
realized. Now there are two rooftop gardens: a hothouse for
growing new plantings and an open-air garden where vegetables,
tomatoes, herbs, and flowers are grown to completion.

The area formed by the two shipping containers is now
joined to the main building, creating an indoor-outdoor dining
room in the middle. Behind it all, beyond a wooden fence that
is open only to staff and for special events, a large courtyard
opens up where the owners have constructed an outdoor pizza
oven, bread oven, wood storage, and potting shed to support
the many activities the group spearheads, from pizza- and bread-
making classes to weddings.

One of the many elements that convey the hands-on, do-it-
yourself manner in which Roberta's came into being is a blackboard sign hung outside in the back bar area. Guests contribute
chalked messages about their experience at the restaurant. In
terms of what a dining establishment decides to hang on its
walls, this is about as organic as it gets.

ABOVE The outdoor extension of the dining room utilizes the surfaces of two shipping containers as interior wall treatments, with a roof constructed of thick wood beams and corrugated plastic and metal sheeting. Mismatched chairs tuck under custom-made wood-topped tables, and Christmas lights make the space glow at night.

RIGHT A window cut into one of the shipping containers reveals the recording studio for the Heritage Foods USA online radio station, so that the linked endeavors of Heritage Foods and Roberta's can coexist in a practical way.

ABOVE California chef and restaurateur Alice Waters helped to start a rooftop hothouse and open-air garden for Roberta's.

RIGHT Roberta's in-house builder fabricated the mobile pizza oven seen in the background, initially built onto a boat trailer and taken to different events around the city. The oven was craned in from the street. A bread oven stands next to it, the site of pizza- and bread-making classes.

LEFT AND BELOW
A blackboard nailed to
a wall in the back of the
restaurant gives diners
room to doodle messages.

OPPOSITE The hothouse
is kept at temperature
with heat piped up from
the compressor used
to cool the refrigerator
downstairs.

White Box BLANCA

OPPOSITE The
Japanese-inspired
Douglas fir lattice at
the entrance creates
a green wall, which
also holds a hidden
door to the restroom.

BELOW Everything
happening in the
restaurant happens in
one room. The walls are
tiled with pristine-white
oversize subway tiles.
The counter looks onto
an Electrolux kitchen
the owners designed
themselves. When not
being used for the chef's
table, the kitchen
doubles as the production
kitchen for the entire
restaurant group,
including catering.
A large part of the
design hinges on the
space being functional
for up to ten cooks,
and then easily cleaned
in time for Blanca's
service.

What once was a mechanic's shop on the same compound as Roberta's in Bushwick is now Blanca, a chef's table that makes you forget that anything messy ever existed there, inside or out. The space—designed by its owners, Chris Parachini, Brendan Hoy, and chef Carlo Mirarchi, and their in-house builder at the time, Joshua Corey—is as crisp and white as a state-of-the-art kitchen should be.

"We were working in this direction at Roberta's all along but had taken the talents of the chef and his team as far as they could go there," says Parachini. "Everyone knew they still had a lot left to give, so we needed a new venue to showcase that—something that would allow them to stretch the technical aspects of the cooking and showcase the amazing raw product they were working with. This basically began a process of subtraction in design. We began taking away anything and everything that opposed or muddied the diner's observation of and connection with the food, the people making it, and the process, until we were left with something close to a white box."

The team then designed a few interior elements that would make diners comfortable while sitting for three hours and eating several courses, adding warm wood tones to the dining area. They created the captain-chair seats, which were custom-fabricated by a man in Connecticut who builds seats for hot rods. "We went up there, got the angle just right, picked the leather, and then built the bases while we waited for them to come in," Parachini recalls. They chose a soft, caramel-colored leather that coincides with the Douglas fir cabinets on the side wall and the Japanese-inspired lattice near the entrance.

The owners selected the unpolished, usually unseen side of a stock porcelain countertop as the dining surface, which will wear over time. "We think that's good," states Parachini. "We like our restaurants to look lived in."

Modern Nature

VANDERBILT AVENUE

ABOVE Certain portions
of the design open
outward, completing
the connection
between the kitchen
and the backyard.

OPPOSITE The pavilion
turns the garden into
a duplex experience,
with a glass eat-in
kitchen on top and
a peaceful reading
room below.

An extension can be anything, from a continuation of the existing building to something wildly different that provides a surprise, or at least a stark contrast. This is the case with the garden pavilion that Chris McVoy and Beth O'Neill designed for Jed Marcus and Jessica Greenbaum. The row house itself dates to 1874 and the extension to 2010, although in many ways it tips a bit further into the future.

The concept was to create an escape from the house, a perch in the trees. Walking into the extension off the traditional dining room on the parlor level, the sensation is of entering a glass pod that is level with the tree branches outside. Two different types of glass, fogged and clear, create the geometric windows, some of which swing out, and the view through them is nothing like the normal view in a row house backyard. One can see horizontally, across the fences, yards, and trees. McVoy and O'Neill maximized the concept of "stepping out into the garden" by turning it into a duplex.

"We wanted a kitchen close to the rear parlor dining room," says Marcus. "The typical approach is to fit a kitchen inside, but we felt that would be too violent an intrusion into the historically intact parlor floor. We also wanted to preserve the surprise of seeing the garden through the rear parlor window when one opens the front door. Once in the kitchen, we wanted to feel closer to the large, complex oak tree in our garden."

To counter the slick, sharp angles, mahogany was added to the steel frame, giving it warmth and color. The top floor is used as the kitchen, the glass extending below the eat-in countertop. On the bottom floor, Marcus and Greenbaum wanted to keep the roughened exterior wall of the existing building exposed, bringing a distressed-stone texture into the mix.

Inside the main house, the challenge was to preserve an area of the parlor level that did not look into the very-modern extension. From the entry hallway, then, the view through the right half of the building has been left intact. The surprise comes when looking through the left half of the formal dining room, past the traditional door trim and into a truly modern pavilion.

The kitchen features two walls of shaped glass panes trimmed with steel and mahogany, black silestone countertops, and a ceramic tile floor. The room attaches to the historical parlor floor, yet stands apart. Rather than attempt to blend the new addition with the main house, the owners decided to juxtapose them.

LEFT The view from the entry hall does not convey the modern surprise one will find in the back of the house.

BELOW A floating red-oak staircase leads down to the lower level, which houses a space for reading as well as a family room. The building's exterior wall extends here as well, and McVoy and O'Neill designed specially notched red-oak doors dividing the two rooms.

INNOVATION / FORT GREENE

Stairway to Heaven

S. 4TH STREET

ABOVE Viewed from across the street, the carport gate both continues the facade of the top floors and also produces the effect of a heavy minimalist form floating above a volume of space.

OPPOSITE A Plexiglas hallway on the third floor that connects the kitchen and living room to the master bedroom allows for visibility as well as a fun walk "on air."

In 2005, Standard Architects was hired by an artist to convert a one-story auto body garage in Williamsburg into a three-story dwelling, complete with a studio space and carport on the ground floor and built-out deck on the roof. The collaboration between the client, design team, and builder transformed the existing building into an utterly contemporary townhouse. The result is a feat of engineering and design not normally seen in an urban residence.

The great architectural idea behind the house is the ground-to-roof stairwell running up the entire right side of the interior, which appears to be exposed to the roof. Upon walking in, the triple-height ceiling causes a moment of awe, as the first thing one sees is the sky fifty feet up through skylights running the depth of the building.

While designing, the Standard team wanted to take advantage of the open space provided by an adjacent schoolyard behind the house, so they created large windows facing the yard to the north and smaller openings on the front of the building, facing the street. To bring more natural light into the interior spaces, then, the architects proposed the stairwell, which cuts through all three floors and is glassed in by skylights on the roof and tall windows on the facades of the building. The concept was to let light bounce around in the voluminous cavity and enter the interior spaces through purposefully arranged openings onto the stairwell.

Terraces extend off the second and third floors: the second-floor terrace functioning as a playground for the artist's children as well as a wall garden, and the narrower third-floor deck as a place to sit and grill something for dinner. For real al fresco dining, the L-shaped roof deck provides a long dining area, as well as a Jacuzzi sunk into a raised wood platform.

From the dining room, one can look through a cutout
in the wall onto the concrete treads of the stairs leading
to the roof, which appear to dangle in space. In fact,
the steps have been fixed to the cutout with steel rods.

LEFT The master bed-
room window frames the
slant of the subway train
as it makes its slight as-
cent over the Williams-
burg Bridge.

BOTTOM LEFT AND RIGHT
From the master bed-
room itself, one has the
sense of floating, as it is
possible to see up and
down through space at
the same time.

INNOVATION / **WILLIAMSBURG**

ABOVE On the roof,
a fully built deck and
Jacuzzi look out onto
the rooftops and the
Williamsburg Bridge.

BELOW The terrace yard off the second floor has been made kid-friendly with recycled-rubber mats to provide a softer surface to play on. The back wall is made with painted steel sheets. The silhouette cutouts are magnetic, allowing the children to rearrange them. The wall garden grows in containers made from folded aluminum, fabricated by a shop that makes gutters.

Garden Minimum

SIDNEY PLACE GARDEN

The garden in this Brooklyn Heights residence strikes a balance between concrete and wood, gray and green, formality and playfulness. Landscape architect Susannah Drake brought a modern aesthetic to this backyard space in line with the airy openness and clean edges of the townhouse interior.

On one side, Drake installed a black concrete wall that acts as a cascading fountain by capturing excess rainwater in channels built into the rim. The recycled fountain water is then used to irrigate the perimeter plantings, ensuring that the garden is not only aesthetically pleasing but also environmentally sustainable.

The other walls of the garden are built of reclaimed teak, inserting a natural element between the dark gray stone and lush greenery throughout. The teak has been incorporated into a raised arbor in the back corner, a structure built of stainless steel and glass to provide subtle amounts of shade. Drake added a playful chain-mail curtain to the arbor, softening it as well as providing extra privacy. A two-person swing offers seating for kids and adults alike.

Stainless steel and glass are then repeated in the exterior staircase connecting the garden and parlor levels. In fact, the balcony off the parlor-level kitchen has a glass floor, allowing light to penetrate to the garden below. It is this perfectly balanced composition of beige-colored raked gravel, dark gray stone, and steel in the design that vibrantly offsets the rich greens of the mosses and other plantings.

ABOVE The stainless-steel and mirror screen Landscape designer Susannah Drake designed for the privacy wall outside of the kitchen provides visual excitement and echoes the arbor materials.

OPPOSITE Drake pared down the elements in this minimalist yet vivid townhouse garden.

RIGHT Green moss—a mixture of cushion, hair cap, sheet, and rock cap mosses—is part of every detail in the patio stone, softening, just a bit, the geometry of the design.

LEFT The raised arbor in the back of the garden provides a place set apart as well as an area for the owners' children to play.

RIGHT The chain-mail curtain offers a soft metallic solution to creating privacy in the arbor. It is also a fun accoutrement for the family's children, who like to stage plays. The glass beams help to deflect the sun's rays and keep the light pleasant without blocking it out.

Drake designed a laser-cut stainless-steel and
mirror screen for the privacy wall outside of
the kitchen. The glass floor of the balcony lets
light through to the garden below.

Inside Out

SUNSET PARK MATERIALS RECYCLING FACILITY

OPPOSITE Every element
of the Recycling
Center's buildings,
including the metal
cladding on the
Tipping Building, was
pre-engineered using
recycled materials.

BELOW The Tipping
Building, which receives
recyclables by barge,
provides a striking
example of how Selldorf
Architects expressed
the support structure
of the pre-engineered
buildings outside of the
cladding.

In 2013 the City of New York and Sims Municipal Recycling opened the largest recycling center in the United States. Poised on the Brooklyn waterfront, the Sunset Park Materials Recycling Facility receives the city's metal, glass, and plastic recyclables mostly by barge, reducing the amount of truck travel on city streets. Blazing the trail for other sustainable initiatives, it incorporates the largest application of solar panels in New York City and wind-turbine power, as well as storm water management with bio-swales and a collection pond.

Selldorf Architects created an overall master plan for the site to respond to the functional components of the Recycling Center's program. The design, on an eleven-acre pier, devotes 36 percent of the property to new open green space and provides distinct circulation systems for trucks and visitors as well as bike and pedestrian travel. Reused concrete and asphalt from the existing site make up the fill, along with crushed recycled glass and mole rock from the construction of the new 2nd Avenue subway tunnel in Manhattan.

The buildings themselves—a tipping building where recyclables arrive by barge and truck, a processing building, a bale storage building, and the visitor center and administration building—are pre-engineered using recycled material. One of the design challenges was to find ways to articulate what the Recycling Center does while giving an overall expression to the design that would distinguish it from typical big-box construction. Normally, pre-engineered structures are simple boxes without much architectural articulation, but for the tipping building the architects essentially turned the building inside out, placing the structural columns and large cross braces on the outside to give it dynamism.

Selldorf Architects had never undertaken a structure like this before, but the firm immediately seized the opportunity to conceive an infrastructure building that contributes to the visual landscape of the city.

Theatrical Leaps and Bounds BAM FISHER

Judith and Alan Fishman Space

ABOVE The main lobby, which has polished concrete floors and aluminum-wrapped columns, doubles as an exhibition space. The painting shown, *Gesture Performing Dance, Dance Performing Gesture*, was created in mixed media by local artist José Parlá.

OPPOSITE Wide stairs leading up to the Rita K. Hillman Studio change color and reflect in the glass railing, extending and playing upon the linear elements in the space.

The Brooklyn Academy of Music's first new building in more than a century was completed in 2012, designed by H3 Hardy Collaboration Architecture. The 40,000-square-foot, seven-story structure was conceived on the site of the Salvation Army's former Brooklyn Citadel Corps, around the corner from BAM's Peter Jay Sharp Building.

H3 utilized the 1928 Salvation Army facade and extended a modern version on top, forming a complementary brick box set back from the street. Landmarks required that the extension be a background building rather than one that approached or cantilevered over the sidewalk. Another challenge was to match as closely as possible the color and mortar of the original brick.

While the facade in general had to be preserved, the architects' great achievement was to open it up. During the neighborhood's harder times in the 1970s and '80s, the facade had become fortressed: the arched doorways and many windows had been bricked in or covered. H3 reestablished the arched entrances and inserted glass doors to make the building welcoming to theatergoers and passersby. The addition of glass wherever possible also reveals BAM Fisher's many activities, bringing it to life.

By contrast, BAM Fisher's interior is completely modern. For the performance spaces, H3 instigated some of the most cutting-edge thinking in theater design. The intimate and flexible Judith and Alan Fishman Space seats 250 people and is designed to accommodate a range of performance and art forms as well as audience arrangements. According to the artist's vision, the seats can be reconfigured in relation to the stage and even removed altogether. The theater also demonstrates the latest in lighting design, with a tension grid attached to the ceiling that can be adjusted for different lighting and drop-scenery installations. Then on the third floor, the 1,600-square-foot Rita K. Hillman Studio, which has large picture-window views of Brooklyn, can be converted into a second performance space.

The building was designed for LEED Gold Certification, implementing more efficient lighting and air-conditioning systems—sources of energy theaters typically overuse—as well as a green roof. As the Brooklyn Academy of Music is one of the borough's central arts institutions, it seems only right that it should lead the charge in creating forward-thinking and energy-efficient performance spaces. Going to an arts performance will never be the same.

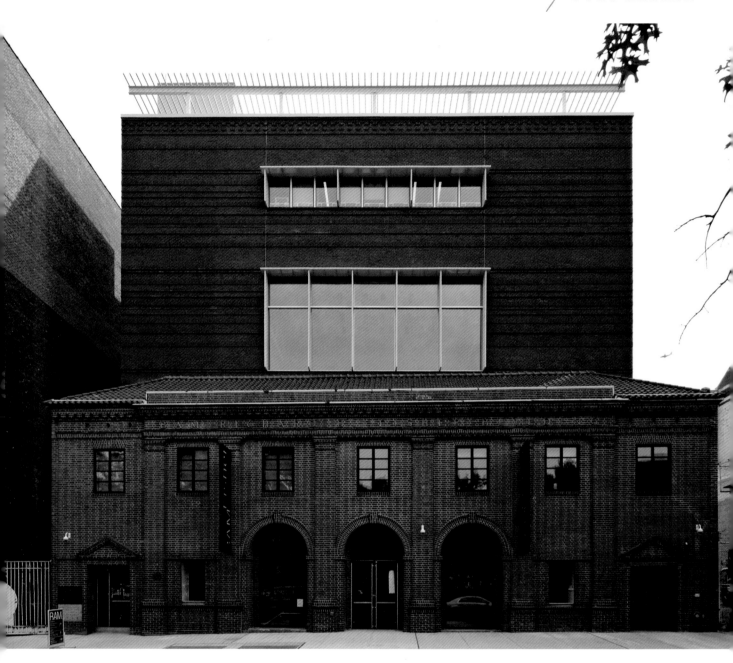

ABOVE The facade of
the BAM Fisher retains
the original arched
doorways and column
decoration, just as the
square modern extension
allows the original
1928 roofline to show.
The cornice trim on the
addition echoes the
original.

ABOVE The seating for 250 in the Judith and Alan Fishman Space is customizable so that artists can shape the theater to their needs. A hanging grid for lighting can be adjusted for all types of scenery installations. Even the air-conditioning units are movable. A walkway on the grid is used as a teaching area.

LEFT The railings in the Fishman Space were laser-cut from imagery of Brooklyn street maps.

Infinite Glamour

FLAVOR PAPER RESIDENCE

ABOVE Adopted from a parking garage, Flavor Paper's headquarters has a preserved shell that has been painted black on the facade.

OPPOSITE Jon Sherman decorated the interior walls of the 65-foot-high periscope that runs up the height of the Flavor Paper building with pink and purple neon tubes.

Jon Sherman, founder of the wallpaper and textiles company Flavor Paper, has a lifelong love of infinity mirrors. The facade of his Boerum Hill headquarters hints at this; if you happen upon it at night, the partially exposed stairwell glows pink and purple, the result of decorative neon tubes lighting a 65-foot-high periscope. Sherman created the design for the building—which houses both the wallpaper printing operation as well as his residence—with his friend Jeff Kovel of Skylab Architecture in Portland, Oregon. Housing both a thriving business and its owner's sense of play and creativity, the design reflects years of hard work as well as fun.

Kovel opened up the building's dilapidated interiors and transformed them into a ground-floor printing factory, a sleek showroom and office level, a third floor with two employee apartments, and a penthouse residence for Sherman. In Sherman's apartment, not a single surface has been left undone: the ceilings of the kitchen and dining rooms, which one first encounters, have been shaped into mock-crocodile-coated arches. The effect is softening and intimate, while the purpose of the arches was also functional (they mask the ductwork without having to drop the entire ceiling in a uniform way, and they add considerable sound advantages). The outcome gives the sensation of walking into a confined space only to take a few steps and enter a wide-open expanse of living room.

The reason for this expansiveness is the far wall, which is made entirely of glass and slides open. Separated from the outside world only by a glass French balcony, the opening provides an exhilarating juxtaposition to the plushly carpeted interior. Sherman loves surprises, and there are others more subtly placed throughout that have a lot to do with mirrors. Mirrored walls in the kitchen and living room also create a sense of infinite space.

To say Sherman's residence is an ode to texture is perhaps an understatement. Not a single element reveals drywall. Upstairs, Sherman kept most of the roof deck a grassy, wildflower-filled meadow. Looking over the railing on the south end of the building, the same side that in Sherman's apartment completely opens to the elements, one sees the quiet, lush backyards of neighboring townhouses. It's a view that reminds Sherman of New Orleans, where he lived for many years: the surprise of a garden one finds in the city, when all you are used to seeing is the street.

RIGHT Music is a steady part of Sherman's life; often album covers inspire his wallpaper designs. The DJ booth's walls are a custom Flavor Paper print of a Mardi Gras Indian scene from his Treme neighborhood in New Orleans. A trombone sits poised on the edge of the counter. Hanging microphone lights by Re-Surface, based in Brooklyn, fit right in. The stools are Miura stools by Konstantin Grcic.

BELOW Mock-crocodile arches in the kitchen keep the room feeling enclosed and intimate, while mirrored walls give it added spaciousness.

ABOVE Sherman and Kovel designed the interiors as a team, including the tinted-glass dining table and light fixture. Tom Dixon candelabras grace the room. Blended in with the contemporary features are significant pieces of 1950s and '60s high design, such as the William Katavalos "T" dining chairs.

RIGHT The mirror-like surfaces of both the table and fixture reflect a grid of golden lights, creating an infinity-mirror illusion in the tabletop itself.

The far wall of the living room is made entirely of glass and
slides open at the push of a button. Sherman has lived in New
Orleans, and still travels there on business to Flavor Paper's textile
headquarters, and so brass instruments reminiscent of second
lines play a role in certain interior moments. A wall sculpture,
the *Shermaphone*, which Sherman created out of trumpets,
saxophones, French horns, and trombones, hangs above the living
room couch designed by Kovel and Sherman. The floors, both
wood and carpeting, were installed by the Floor Group in Georgia.
The wood itself comes from river-reclaimed cypress from Louisiana
and has been given a dark stain.

ABOVE High modern
does not necessarily
mean hard-edged in this
apartment, and the
master bedroom is proof
of this. With faux-fur
carpeting that then rolls
up onto the wall behind
the bed, the room is
filled with softness.

RIGHT The Sheba ceiling
paper, an entrancing
illustrative representation
of white fur, echoes
the soft furlike carpet
in the room.

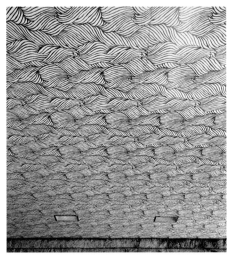

Sherman's master bath
has fun with black
features sparked by
hot-pink accents,
harkening back to
the building's facade.

Garage Expressions

HOT BIRD

ABOVE Hot Bird is situated just off of Atlantic Avenue, where drivers have a plethora of auto body shops to choose from. Owner Frank Moe utilized an arrow sign he found in Tennessee for the entrance and painted the exterior of the original garage door, which is kept closed.

RIGHT The bright-red wooden fence outside Hot Bird protects the outdoor drinking garden from the noise on Atlantic Avenue.

OPPOSITE An antique wood saw provides a place to set drinks.

Even an auto body shop can become a popular watering hole, given an innovative conversion. The bar Hot Bird beautifully integrates its past as a garage with its new life. Owner Frank Moe kept the shell intact and barely cleaned the two garage doors, one of which had been filled in with glass bricks. He decided to create a storefront in one of the other openings, the way it would have appeared in 1930. Just outside, a brassy-red wooden fence protects the bar's al fresco seating from the noise of Atlantic Avenue, one of Brooklyn's busiest boulevards.

Moe gathered salvaged pieces from a variety of places, including two wood saws from Baltimore, which he placed in the center of the room, providing extra surfaces for drinks when it gets crowded. He placed a wood planer behind the bar, setting the cash register on top of it.

"In terms of the design of the place, I did all of the research and made all the decisions alone," says Moe. "I talked to a lot of my friends, running ideas by them, mostly trying to figure out the layout of the place, where people would sit, stand, walk, and feel comfortable. The bar on one hand feels 'real' to me, because there are so many 'mistakes' and unfinished, unpolished things. It somehow feels natural, almost alive because it has a past."

With high ceilings and machine elements that seem left over from the space's auto body days even though they were consciously selected for the bar, Hot Bird's interior completes its mission of repurposing an old garage as a contemporary gathering place.

ABOVE Moe found these replicas of the Toledo factory stools at Restoration Hardware, just as he was trying to locate originals on eBay and in various antique shops.

LEFT Moe tracked down old machine-shop tables and benches all along the East Coast and created communal seating with them.

OPPOSITE TOP Two antique wood saws add to the aesthetic.

OPPOSITE LEFT The garage lights fit perfectly in the space, although they were not original to the building. Moe found them at a salvage shop in Washington, D.C.

OPPOSITE RIGHT Moe left the garage doors in place, adding seating along the perimeter.

Contemporary Culmination WAVERLY AVENUE

ABOVE AND OPPOSITE
The fourteen-foot-wide house was initially one of four identical dwellings for "ferriers" to the mansions on Clinton and Washington Avenues. The facade has been restored to its original brick. The front door was restored by a carpenter in the Navy Yard. Owner-architect David Hecht keeps a model of the house on a bookshelf.

What was once a city-condemned building in slowly gentrifying Clinton Hill is now a light-filled three-story home situated in one of Brooklyn's most sought-after neighborhoods. Its owners, architect David Hecht, principal of David Hecht Architecture, and his wife, Liz Thorpe, had hunted for a house that was affordable, which by default meant a structure in such bad shape they could really make it their own. When they purchased the 1860s building at auction at Borough Hall, Hecht had already begun designing, so that within a few weeks they were ready to begin.

At that point, Hecht had professionally worked only on new construction and knew little about old buildings; he was a committed modernist when he began his own house project. The job was much harder than he had anticipated, but he soon discovered that there are important benefits to old buildings.

"What came through to me was this latent interest I had in the narrative power of architecture," he says, "the idea that the architecture and our environment around us tells a story over time." The finished renovation reveals a front that is more traditional than the back. As you move through, the building opens up and the details become more contemporary.

The biggest challenge was to get light into the middle of the house. One of four identical dwellings for "ferriers," horse-and-buggy drivers for the grand mansions on Clinton and Washington Avenues, the building is only fourteen feet wide. But Hecht quickly realized that fourteen feet, in fact, provided the ideal dimension for a room. Although originally families would divide the space into living on the first floor and sleeping on the two floors above, he felt this created a house out of balance. In order to capture more space for the public part of the residence, he split the bottom two levels to create visual and spatial continuity between these floors, lowering the kitchen floor half a flight and the second floor half a flight. The result is a balanced home, with three rooms for living and three rooms for sleeping.

Standing in the more traditional front parlor, one can see down onto a modern kitchen as well as up one half-flight into the living room, which now has the eleven-foot ceiling height of a classic townhouse.

LEFT Pink-and-cream Flavor Paper wallpaper, called City Park, invokes the 1860s parlor room, complete with the original marble fireplace, while still giving a playful wink to contemporary sensibilities.

BELOW Light penetrates the house from the back because there are no walls to block it. From the front door, one can see all the way out into the green backyard.

OPPOSITE The extension was added on in the late nineteenth century to house plumbing and was completely dilapidated when the couple took possession. Because its utility had vanished, Hecht felt he could replace it with a clean conscience, keeping the original footprint, as it is landmarked, but reimagining its use and character in a modern way.

BELOW Hecht designed the fireplace and commissioned 4th State Metals in Brooklyn to fabricate it out of sealed raw steel.

OPPOSITE Hecht conceived a modern steel staircase and had it fabricated and installed by AJ Ironworks in Brooklyn. He sealed and finished the metal with a blend of linseed oil and beeswax. The solid red-oak treads and banister, a warm counterpoint to the industrial look of the steel, were fabricated and installed by Adam Wilk, Inc., and are stained with Rubeo Monocoat Oil, in mahogany. Hecht inserted glass guardrails in four places along the stairs instead of a railing to allow for maximum visibility and light.

Material Protests

PACIFIC STREET

ABOVE **Jeff Sherman used copper rolls, ordinarily installed as flashing on roofs, to wrap the coat closet in the entry hall. He wanted to define the volume as an object, which continues upstairs into the office and guestroom.** "It became important to use or not to use certain materials because of what I was trying to say about the shapes."

"Removing a floor is one of those ideas that would be really hard to sell to a client," says owner-architect Jeff Sherman, who finished renovating his duplex Prospect Heights house in 2011. "Square footage is everything in New York." The home Sherman designed for himself became the perfect experiment: he could explore different architectural concepts in a way he might not have the freedom to do in a client's residence. And, if successful, he could bring the results to future projects.

Sherman removed the middle section of the second floor, creating a void in the center of the house. This gave him two important elements: light, from a skylight that he inserted in the roof; and spatial excitement—something row houses don't often have a lot of—with a dramatic, double-height dining room. A catwalk connects the master bedroom on the second floor to the guest bedroom and office on the other side of the void, and Sherman designed a console to act as the railing. From here, one looks over the console onto the dining room below. Suddenly, what would normally be a closed-off space becomes an exciting place to be.

Besides removing part of the second floor, the riskiest decisions Sherman made had to do with surface materials; there are very few areas of drywall in the house. Most are unconventional, a feasible choice because he started from scratch (the building had been used as a dog kennel by the previous owner and had to be gutted and reroofed), but equally driven by his determination to let the architectural elements in the house express themselves through materials.

For example, Sherman covered the walls that encase the shoe storage and coat closet near the front door with horizontal copper sheets, installed like clapboards. "The copper was a material decision to clarify both the shape and what the shape meant," says Sherman. "If it was covered in Sheetrock, you would have understood it as another wall of the room."

After demolition, Sherman wanted to preserve the feeling of being able to see all the way through the house, yet still produce a finished space. The corrugated plastic on the master bedroom wall was one way to do this. In fact, the void creates unexpected views throughout the house—onto the sidewalk from the catwalk, out to the sky from the bedroom. By taking one innovative step, a design can trigger so many unexpected gifts.

The inspiration to use copper came from Sherman's travels in Europe and his admiration for the bronze statues one finds in almost every plaza. Where tourists touch the statue, the material remains shiny. The original marble fireplace in the living room was hidden under a dozen layers of paint.

ABOVE Since he was building much of the house himself, Sherman had to find materials that he could install easily. He chose cedar planks, traditionally used as closet lining, for the ceiling on the first floor. For the skylight, Sherman designed a monitor with a vertical window cut into it, an opening that brings in low winter light during colder months while keeping higher, hotter summer rays out, and positioned it flush with the outside wall of the bedroom. Light streams in to illuminate the semitranslucent material, which is corrugated plastic, and the entire house glows.

RIGHT Sherman ran the corrugated plastic of the master bedroom wall up into the monitor that houses the skylight.

The floors on the
second level are the
original wide-plank
subfloor stained dark.

ABOVE AND RIGHT There
was tin wainscoting
along the stairs when
Sherman bought the
house. He found raw
pressed tin to match and
installed it as a
backsplash in the
kitchen. The pantry
doors double as
blackboard for writing
down grocery lists.

OPPOSITE Concrete
parging is not normally
used as a finishing
technique, but here it
makes a beautiful
surface and spans two
stories on one wall.
"I hadn't planned on
parging the walls when
I bought the house, but
once we opened them
up and saw the awful
condition of the masonry,
parging was a structural
and an aesthetic solution."

Rooftop Bounty

BOND STREET VEGETABLE GARDEN

ABOVE Colorful small flowerpots enliven the brick wall.

OPPOSITE Foras Studio surrounded the planters with artificial grass to create a play space for Casale's son and to add texture and warmth to the area. The black dining table and chairs are from West Elm. The white chairs are from Ikea.

RIGHT The beauty of this rooftop garden is that it is simple and well-organized as well as abundantly useful. The planters produce everything from fresh eggplants to raspberries to numerous herbs.

Dawn Casale, who founded One Girl Cookies in Brooklyn, dreamed of a terrace vegetable garden where she could have ready access to whatever produce she desired. She hired Susan Welti and Paige Keck of Foras Studio to design a sustainable garden on top of a garage extension attached to her home in Boerum Hill. The walled space sits just off the kitchen, making it accessible while cooking and ideal for entertaining.

Tidy, simple wooden planters align themselves on a vibrant patch of artificial grass. Stepping out, guests feel as though they have entered a professional garden in miniature. Casale grows vegetables, fruits, and herbs, and has also installed three small apple trees, their branches trained to run horizontally along the railing, adding further privacy.

Before the transformation, the area was concrete—more a garage roof than an outdoor space. A single French door opens onto three steps leading down to the kitchen. Nothing could be easier here than stepping outside or stepping in, with arms full of greens.

Architecture as Landscape

BROOKLYN BOTANIC GARDEN VISITOR CENTER

ABOVE WEISS/MANFREDI designed the Visitor Center with patterned glass as well as shaded outdoor passageways, which keep the building cool and counteract bird collisions.

OPPOSITE The wall material in the palm-leaf-shaped Lillian and Amy Goldman Atrium was made from ginkgo wood salvaged at the site.

Since its establishment in 1910, the Brooklyn Botanic Garden has provided fifty-two acres of green space in the middle of a dense urban environment. More than a century later in 2012, due to increased attendance and the need for more visible exhibition areas, the Botanic Garden opened a new entrance and visitor center that demonstrate in every way how architecture can pay tribute to and live within an existing landscape. The center also provides for itself by implementing cutting-edge, environmentally sustainable features.

Designed by New York-based architects Marion Weiss and Michael Manfredi, principals of WEISS/MANFREDI Architecture/Landscape/Urbanism, the structure was conceived as a new threshold between the city and the garden, shifting from an architectural presence on the street to an interactive topography of graceful white columns and spacious windows leading to the grounds. Although a master plan for the project called for an entrance behind the McKim, Mead, and White-designed Brooklyn Museum, WEISS/MANFREDI proposed bringing the garden to the street, inviting in passersby from the sidewalk on Washington Avenue, which runs along the property.

"We are very interested in the reciprocal relationships between landscape and architecture," says Weiss, who grew up in California and was taken to the Brooklyn Botanic Garden on her very first visit. Manfredi is from Italy but moved to Brooklyn at the beginning of what he calls its "renaissance," which he related to as an architect. "Just as the Garden inspires wandering, we designed the Center so that it is never seen in its entirety but is experienced cinematically as an unfolding place of discovery," the principals say about their design.

The 20,000-square-foot Visitor Center offers interpretive exhibits and a room for orienting tour groups, as well as a multiuse event space and a garden store. A geoexchange system consisting of twenty-eight thermal wells dug into the earth below assist in the heating and cooling of the building. WEISS/MANFREDI installed pattern-fritted window glass, which minimizes heat from direct sunlight and prevents bird collisions; the American Bird Conservancy has used the project as a case study. These features and the way the architects used the berm in the existing landscape—nestling the building against the hillside to increase insulation—help to meet the center's energy needs.

ABOVE The living roof of the Visitor Center is planted with 40,000 diverse plants chosen to expand the types of species grown on green roofs. Specialized plantings capture and direct rainwater to reduce the load on the city's storm water management system and to supplement irrigation.

WEISS/MANFREDI designed a 10,000-square-foot living roof for the Visitor Center, cultivated with 40,000 different plants, including grasses, spring bulbs, and perennial wildflowers, many of them native. Both a structural and a natural part of the landscape, the roof will change with the seasons and thus alter the architecture itself. As land, it acts to counter the heat-island effect that results from paved urban surfaces, and as a space that will continue to be planted for years to come, it offers a unique opportunity for experimentation to determine better methods for growing living rooftops in the city, providing a model for metropolitan green spaces around the world.

Given the international reputation Brooklyn has gained as a place of innovation, the Visitor Center participates in a truly global community. "We have been working together for a number of years and around the world," says Manfredi. "Finally we had a chance to build in our own backyard. Brooklyn more than ever has become an international borough, and so we had a sense that we were building an internationally important institution."

ABOVE Botanic Garden president Scot Medbury brought in Chilean monkey trees from the Andes to be placed in the courtyard adjacent to the atrium, introducing a plant element that echoes the more structured nature of the new building. Medbury explains that sensitivity to the existing landscape and the necessity of incorporating environmentally sustainable features both beautifully and meaningfully were the top priorities for the project. "As with anything built today, this should be the first question," he says.

Brooklyn industry is booming in the early twenty-first century. After sitting dormant for decades, old factory and warehouse spaces have lit up again as developers large and small realize the benefits of repurposing postindustrial buildings. The Brooklyn Navy Yard has led the way in industrial job growth by converting nineteenth-century shipyard buildings and introducing ground-up green construction. The collaborative facility New Lab at the Navy Yard takes part of an 1899 ship hangar to provide shared design and fabrication space for institutions and entrepreneurs alike.

In addition, in Dumbo, Red Hook, Williamsburg, and Gowanus, furniture, lighting, and textile designers can find affordable space in which to compose ideas, make their products, and prepare them for the marketplace. Because of proximity to one another, makers can share ideas and solutions in a way that improves output and builds community. Collective woodshops in Bushwick and Clinton Hill allow entrepreneurs to practice and perfect their trade. High-tech machinery has also been introduced into these old spaces. Textile makers work from looms connected to computers, merging past and present techniques to create vibrant patterns and textures.

Brooklyn has generated a community of artisans and entrepreneurs for decades—now these businesses can find even more room and reason to grow in their own backyard.

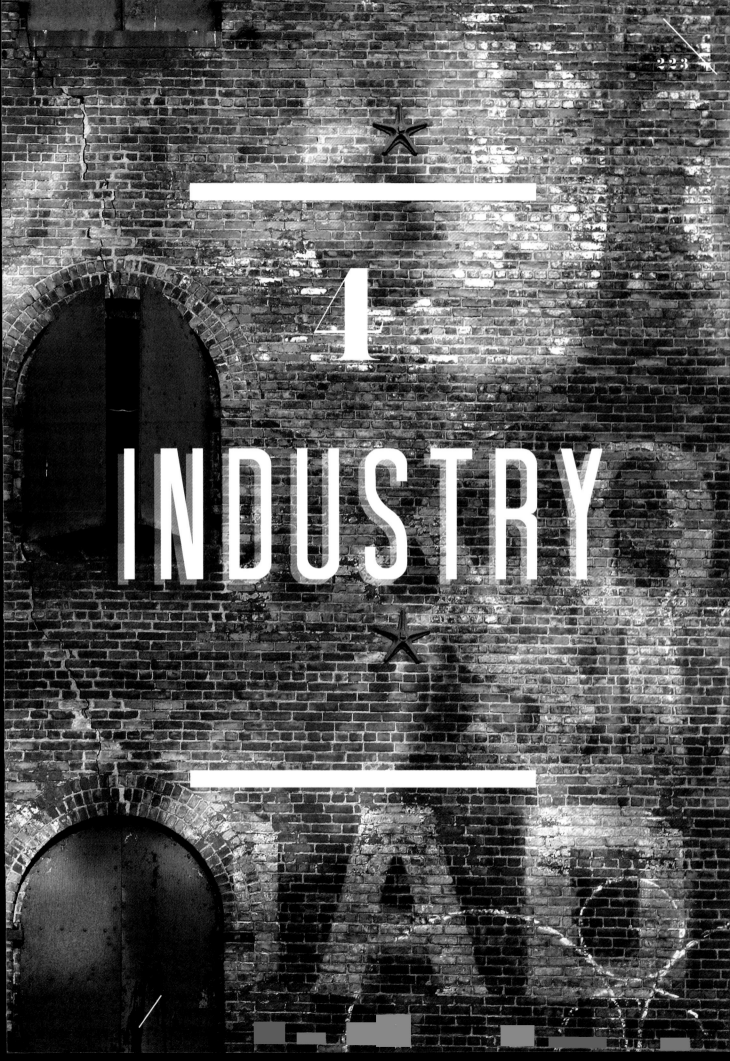

4

INDUSTRY

Redefining Modern Manufacturing

BROOKLYN NAVY YARD

ABOVE "Adaptive reuse of old buildings is the greenest thing you can do," states Kimball. "We renovated the Paymaster Building understanding that if you bring an old building back to life and preserve its history, innovative businesses will come. Kings County Distillery uses the space now."

The Brooklyn Navy Yard was established in 1801, and the Navy built ships there for more than 150 years. When the Navy pulled out in 1966, what had been the epicenter of American manufacturing for decades was reduced to a near-empty space only partially used for private shipbuilding.

"When the Navy left the Yard, it was a traumatic time for Brooklyn and the city," says Andrew Kimball, president of the Brooklyn Navy Yard Development Corporation (BNYDC). "There was 'white flight' to the suburbs, and massive loss of manufacturing jobs to the South and the Midwest and then increasingly abroad."

The Navy base went from peak employment during World War II of 70,000 people to a nadir of a thousand people. The city bought the property in 1969 with the intent of reviving it to solve many of the city's employment problems. They first sought out other large-scale manufacturers, such as the automobile and handbag industries, aiming to rekindle the days of big manufacturing, but those days were gone. In the mid 1980s, Mayor Ed Koch created the Brooklyn Navy Yard Development Corporation (BNYDC), a not-for-profit entity with a fresh vision for the Yard.

"They get a lot of credit for turning the tide," Kimball explains. "The first thing they did was to realize that they could never again be reliant on one big industry. Even in the mid eighties, there were already the seeds of this artisanal, light-industrial growth popping up around Brooklyn, and what they realized was that the real estate product that didn't exist was one that was very small, where a tenant could come in at a decent industrial rent. The BNYDC started to cut up these buildings into smaller units, and so initiated a new leasing strategy."

In the late 1990s, BNYDC presented its new business model to the Bloomberg administration: to target sectors that have long-term viability in the city, at the same time redefining what modern manufacturing is. With city, state, and federal funds for subsurface infrastructure like plumbing and electricity, the BNYDC developed a private model for repurposing old shipyard buildings and constructing, from the ground up,

Workshop/apd designed an aluminum screen for the facade of BLDG 92, punched with holes based on a blown-up image of the launching of the USS *Brooklyn* in 1936. The screen lets natural light through but keeps the building cooler than it would be with an exposed glass facade.

ABOVE Duggal Visual Solutions has made the Brooklyn Navy Yard its home for multiple decades and so it was natural that

Duggal Energy Solutions should follow suit. The former shipbuilding facilities provide the breadth of space for founder Baldev Duggal to realize his vision of an ecotech campus, beginning with the Duggal Greenhouse (shown here), a building that showcases sustainable design and also acts as an event space. Powered by renewable sources including solar and natural gas, high-efficiency fans and lighting keep the interior ventilated and efficiently lit.

LEFT Lumi-Solair, which makes Duggal's Lumi-Solair street lamps, is also based in the Navy Yard, which, due to the lack of underground wiring, provided the perfect testing ground. The lights implement solar panels and wind turbines to collect power in a battery stored in the base of the lamppost, which operates an energy-efficient LED bulb. Because there is no need for pole-to-pole conduits and wiring, Lumi-Solair lights contribute major installation savings.

ABOVE LEFT **BLDG 92** was designed by Beyer Blinder Belle Architects & Planners and workshop/apd and manufactured in the Navy Yard as modular units. It incorporates the 1850s Marine Commandant's House as a museum.

ABOVE RIGHT The Brooklyn Navy Yard demonstrates how 200-year-old shipyard buildings can operate side by side with new construction.

BELOW The BNYDC put in the city's first mounted wind turbines on the Perry Building.

environmentally sound structures. By leasing the buildings to arts and culture, entertainment and media, high-end home goods, and design-driven manufacturing businesses, the Navy Yard has once again become a place where different sectors work side by side to design and fabricate, providing a remarkable model for revitalizing urban manufacturing.

"The Brooklyn Navy Yard is the only place in the United States of its kind: a former Naval base converted for its original purpose, which is industrial manufacturing and creativity," says Kimball. "Forty to fifty percent of our tenants are in arts and culture manufacturing and entertainment and media manufacturing. This is all part of figuring out, What is a twenty-first-century manufacturing use that is related to broader economic expansion in New York?"

As BNYDC president, Kimball generated the idea for an exhibition, visitors, and employment center that would tell the story of the Yard's remarkable history as well as show what is happening there in the present. Beyer Blinder Belle Architects & Planners and workshop/apd led the design of BLDG 92, which joins the 1850s Marine Commandant's House with a new green building. Navy Yard tenants participated in the build and contribute to various aspects of the exhibits.

BLDG 92 also provides key services for tenants, such as a café and an employment center, where the BNYDC places twenty people a month in jobs.

The Collaborative Future NEW LAB

New Lab was based on a vision of bringing professional design institutions together in a shared space. David Belt, founder of developer Macro Sea, Inc., worked with 3rd Ward in Bushwick, an early model of a cooperative space for design entrepreneurs. At New Lab, the concept is taken to a whole new level. Seventy-seven thousand square feet of the hangar provide a vast, high-ceilinged interior with expansive windows. Members include world-ranking academic institutions and architecture firms, as well as entrepreneurial design entities. Each has private office and/or studio space but also takes part in shared classrooms and shared access to high-end production equipment: 3-D molding machines, 3-D printers, and water jets.

"The idea is to create a true collective, with no one institution or entity overseeing everyone else," explains Belt. "The interior spaces benefit from adjacency as well as transparency." Macro Sea designed the cathedral-like interior with Rogers Marvel Architects and brought in Maria Aiolova of Terreform ONE as project consultant.

The Brooklyn Navy Yard Development Corporation (BNYDC) realized that it would be ultimately more efficient to reuse the existing hangar, built for shipbuilding in 1899, than to take it down. Not only was repurposing less expensive; it provided a context in which designers wanted to work. As BNYDC president Andrew Kimball explains, "A big reason tenants were interested in the hangar was the historic building itself, the vibe and the message that it sends."

MACRO SEA

DESIGNERS IN THEIR STUDIOS

For makers, Brooklyn offers an exceptional place in which to create and set up a company: it provides room in which to work as well as access to one of the largest international marketplaces. The designers showcased here represent a sampling of the many fine creators working in the borough today.

WÜD FURNITURE DESIGN

CLINTON HILL

Corey Springer did not train in woodworking, although he studied sculpture in college. He likes to define his furniture and lighting pieces as "functional sculpture." A mix of materials is central to his designs, which he makes in a wide-open auto body garage space converted into a cooperative woodshop. The round Santos Rosewood top on the Brooklyn card table, which has a pale metal-aluminum base, swirls around a central slot for coasters. Springer uses all local lumber sources and finds Brooklyn to be an all-in-one place for creativity and manufacturing.

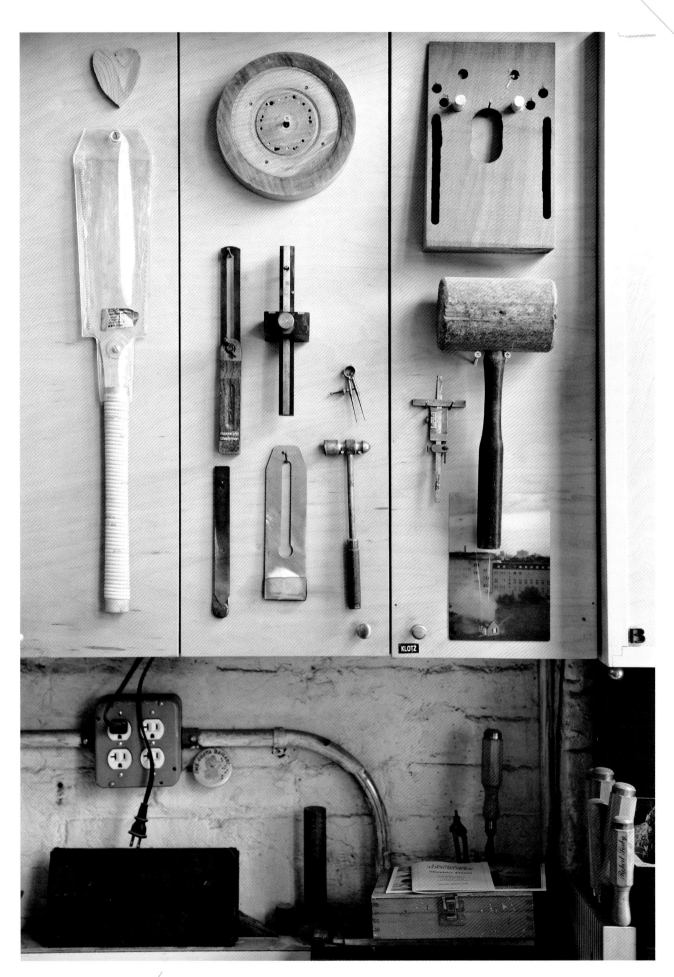

ASWOON/
SUSAN WOODS

BROOKLYN NAVY YARD

Susan Woods, founder of Aswoon, has been
a tenant of the Brooklyn Navy Yard since
1998. A trained sculptor, Woods creates
metal works of varying forms, ranging from
furniture pieces to fine-art wall hangings,
fashioning them out of recycled furniture
springs. She made an early metal piece,
Spring Screen, from the springs of two
pillows a furniture restorer at the Yard had
discarded. The newer Spring Screens, which
are wall hangings, and Spring Screen lounger
both take inspiration from it. Her woodworks,
such as the Black Wave seating, play with
unconventional shapes, implementing bent
wood to create standing screens as well as
ergonomic chairs and benches.

Says Woods, "What people cannot define
in 3-D, they wish to touch. I am very happy
to have ventured into the design world in
part because I have significantly grown as a
creator of 3-D objects."

FERRA DESIGNS

BROOKLYN NAVY YARD

In 2000, founder Rob Ferrarone and his
business partner, Jeff Kahn, established
a 10,000-square-foot metal shop and studio
for Ferra Designs in the Brooklyn Navy Yard.
The space provides room for precision water-
jet cutting equipment, which Ferra uses to
create high-end architectural metalwork
and furniture. As a member of the Navy Yard
community, Ferrarone designed bike racks
and placed them throughout the industrial
yard. The inspiration for the sculptural yet
functional pieces came from looking through
archival material that BLDG 92 curator
Daniella Romano provided. He came across an
image of a ship's hull under construction
and based his design on it. The racks are
simple yet immediately evocative of a ship,
and of the Navy Yard itself. Ferrarone
selected Corten steel for the parts and
connected them with a stainless-steel
binding.

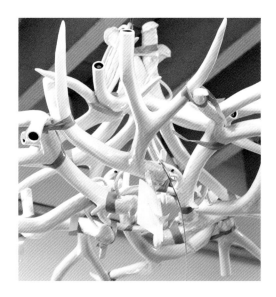

JASON MILLER/ ROLL & HILL

GREENPOINT

Jason Miller introduced his antler chande-
liers early on and now has an assembly line
in his shop in Greenpoint, where the fixtures
are put together and shipped out. He has
established the lighting design company Roll
& Hill, which allows him to create different
lines as well as act as distributor for
other designers such as Lindsay Adelman and
Fort Standard.

MARY WALLIS

BUSHWICK

Mary Wallis is interested in deconstructing
lighting fixtures just as much as she is
in constructing them. The Eadie chandelier
is a perfect example of a design that
explodes the glass panes of a traditional
entry-hall hanging fixture to give a sense
of movement and drama. Wallis likes to
celebrate the crack, she says, and make it
bigger. The chandelier is built of a brass
understructure onto which she has screwed
hand-cut gray-tinted glass panes, some of
which appear to hover around the frame.
Every piece she makes is hands-on because
she builds them all herself.

KATCH DESIGN CO.

WILLIAMSBURG

Pamela and Steph Katch operate a furniture design company alongside their full-service residential interiors firm, Katch I.D., because very often one requires the other. They created the Lucky Beam bench out of the concept of an I beam, cropped to a section and placed on the floor for a versatile seat. As the foundational support of any building, an I beam means stability and support, something the Katch sisters play with by transforming it into an aesthetically pleasing and functional piece for the home. The metal base can be painted in any color. The top is made of reclaimed heart pine.

NIGHTWOOD

WILLIAMSBURG

Ry Scruggs and Nadia Yaron like the fact that furniture has a past life. When deconstructing a chair once, they recognized the beauty of the exposed underside and began making a full range of furnishings that reveal their raw, primitive states. Both Scruggs and Yaron are self-taught and intuit the spiritual essence of the things they make: textiles—which Yaron weaves, dyes, and sews from all-natural materials—and furnishings—which Scruggs builds from refurbished vintage frames or anew from reclaimed wood and other found objects. Each piece is one-of-a-kind, such as a reincarnated vintage chair upholstered with pieces of handmade fabric or a wing chair stripped of its fabric and cushioning to expose the beautiful surfaces of its wood and underpinnings.

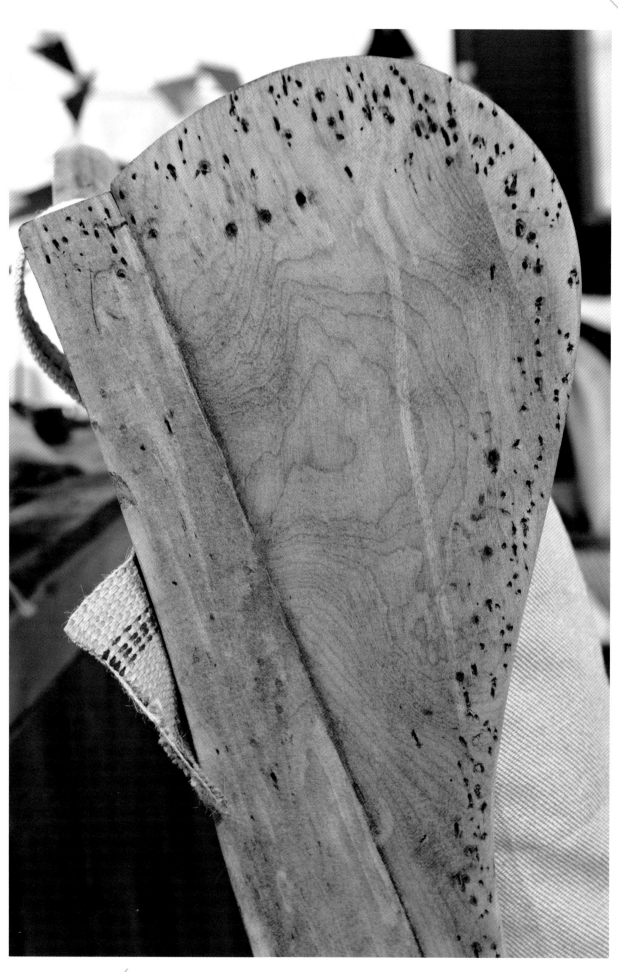

VONNEGUT/KRAFT

SUNSET PARK

Katrina Vonnegut and Brian Kraft combine
complementary interests and talents to
make custom furnishings in a light mix of
materials. While Vonnegut has always been
inspired by textiles and jewelry making,
Kraft is a self-taught carpenter and works
out of a cooperative woodshop in Sunset
Park. The duo designs and builds custom
beds, benches, and other pieces, including
the Maize Bed, with a headboard that
incorporates a graphic slat pattern inspired
by textiles. The Medley bench combines
different woods and finishes, with metal
feet.

EGG COLLECTIVE

CLINTON HILL

Crystal Ellis, Stephanie Beamer, and Hillary
Petrie moved to Brooklyn from points west
and south, choosing it for its affordable
studio space and proximity to the international
marketplace of Manhattan. In 2012, they were
crowned Best New Designer at the International
Contemporary Furniture Fair.

The partners make all of their wood
pieces in a large cooperative shop upstairs
from their showroom, a setup that saves
money for machinery and provides the bonus
of collaborating with others. They source
any parts they can't make, such as stone
and glass, locally. Their designs, which
they describe as "contemporary heirloom
furniture," mix cutting-edge, mid century,
and rustic into one. A prototype for the
Gregory chair juxtaposes fluffy fur-on-hide
cushions with turned white-oak legs. The
egg-shaped Oscar dining table pairs putty-
colored notched travertine marble with a
polished, brass-coated steel geometric base.

TAKESHI MIYAKAWA

GREENPOINT

The work of Takeshi Miyakawa infuses life into inanimate objects, from chairs to shelves to candelabras. Mixing conceptualism with practical design, the output is both humorous and utterly useful. Miyakawa, who trained as an architect, says he did not want to get stuck working behind a desk. At the same time he has an architect's firm grasp on what is possible in design and implements it. His Affordable Housing storage chest is shaped like its namesake to maximize surface area, something useful when drawer space is needed. A candelabra fashioned out of candle wax hangs gracefully over an impromptu walnut-slab dining table rimmed by the designer's Stump chair and 3 x 3 chair. His US Storage shelf—shaped like the American flag—hangs on the wall.

ELASTICCO

GOWANUS

Elodie Blanchard makes curtains and other coverings from a range of embroidered materials. Originally from France, she studied at CalArts before settling in Brooklyn. Her Gowanus studio has a view of the Kentile sign and neighbors the studios of a variety of different designers, artists, and makers. These pillows are covered in 100% wool felt and are machine- and hand-embroidered with bright, sometimes fluorescent, colored thread and cording. Blanchard implements hole punchers and grommets for patterning in many of her creations, such as the parlor and master bedroom drapes she fashioned for Mike Diamond and Tamra Davis's home (pages 75 and 79).

FLAVOR PAPER

BOERUM HILL

Jon Sherman started Flavor Paper—a custom
wallpaper and textiles company—in New
Orleans before seizing the opportunity to
move the wallpaper portion of the business
to Brooklyn. What started as seven original
designs has now grown to more than one
hundred, seven of which have been included
in the permanent collection of the Brooklyn
Museum (one is shown above). The Boerum Hill
headquarters has a ground-floor printing
factory, where all of the papers are made.
Mirrors on the ceiling help determine what
the papers appear like flat as they are
rolled out. Upstairs, clients can peruse
different designs or discuss their own
ideas for a custom paper in the glamorous
showroom. Flavor Paper produces prints
tailored to homes, restaurants, and hotels,
such as the Brooklyn Toile by Mike D (page
80-81) and wallpapers for the Wythe Hotel by
Dan Funderburgh (page 114-115), among others.

HIROKO TAKEDA

DOWNTOWN BROOKLYN

Hiroko Takeda incorporates Japanese weaving
techniques into her throws, tapestries, and
wall coverings. Inspired by the textures,
colors, and materials in fashion season
after season, she mixes visual stimulations
using different materials. A rough waffle
weave has a three-dimensional structure,
especially when woven out of plastic cords,
evoking Western children's lanyard crafts.
The traditional and delicate Japanese leno
weave produces coverings that are light
and airy while stabilizing the fabric at
the same time. Hiroko also likes to use an
embroidery technique common in Bangladesh,
where local people thicken cloth, called
kantha, by making row upon row of tiny
stitches.

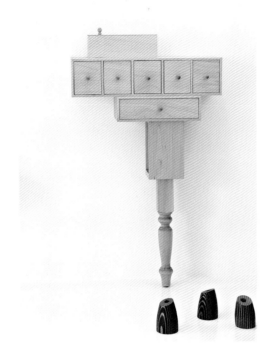

PELLE

RED HOOK

Jean and Oliver Pelle met while studying at
the Yale School of Architecture and have
since made both lighting and furniture
pieces, as well as led interior design
projects, out of their Red Hook studio.
The one-legged entry console was conceived
for the shallow entry halls found in most
modest townhouses and provides a shelf,
drawers, and a lidded box on top convenient
for keeping house keys and other items.
The turned wood candleholders are an early
design of Jean's. A mainstay in their shop
is the Bubble chandelier, which Jean created
as a DIY project originally, clustering airy
glass balls around a central cord of twisted
rope (see pages 57 and 78).

DAVID WEEKS

DUMBO

David Weeks moved to Brooklyn early on,
finding space in Dumbo for a studio to
make furniture and lighting. He has always
designed a full range of objectS but at
one point his lighting pieces took off,
gathering such a following in New York
and beyond that for a while he dedicated
his entire operation to making custom
fixtures. "The trick has been designing
efficient systems," he says. He makes
different arrangements out of the same
parts, producing eight different collections
and forty different styles of lights. The
balance of the parts determines the design
of the finished piece, and so each fixture
is built while hanging to determine the best
configuration. A Kopra Burst in white hangs
in the studio. Weeks inventories all of the
parts for assembly in his Dumbo shop.

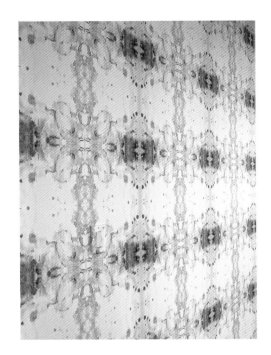

ESKAYEL

WILLIAMSBURG

Shanan Campanaro, who founded her textiles
company, Eskayel, out of her Williamsburg
apartment, creates wallpaper, fabric, and
rug patterns based on her own ink-and-water
paintings. She zooms into one of her works
and selects a detail, which she then mirrors
on computer to create a repeat pattern.
The results are structured patterns that
also hint at the ethereal and primitive
qualities of watercolor, as well as other
influences such as animal figures and
Indonesian imagery. Campanaro has branched
into rug patterns based on the same inky
details, which are woven in India or Nepal
in materials such as aloe and silk.

HELLMAN-CHANG

BUSHWICK

Daniel Hellman and Eric Chang started making
furniture as a hobby, teaching themselves
how to build wooden benches, tables, and
chairs for family members. They worked
nights and weekends until, in 2006, they
won *Interiors Magazine*'s Best of the Year
Design Award for their Z Pedestal table.
A simple concept of a tabletop and base
connected by crossing legs, the table is
crisply modern and organic at the same time.
Hellman-Chang now operates an 11,000-square-
foot woodshop in Bushwick, where they
make all of their furniture and also have
established an organized cooperative of
various entrepreneurs who share machinery,
materials, and ideas.

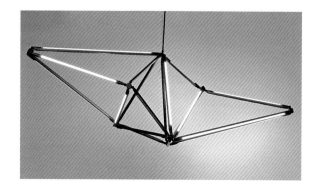

GROW HOUSE GROW!

BUSHWICK

Katie Deedy never trained as a graphic
designer but did major in fine art in
college. She has always found the most
interesting art to have a narrative (her
mother is a professional storyteller),
and has established a textile and design
business, Grow House Grow!, that makes
narrative-driven wallpaper and tiles. Each
grouping of wallpaper patterns has a theme,
and each individual pattern is based on a
story. The Tackapousha wallpaper was created
out of the story of Tackapousha, the Native
American chief who sold the Far Rockaways
and what is now Coney Island to the Dutch.
Deedy interweaves a Native American graphic
with graceful curves reminiscent of turn-
of-the-century luxury hotels, as the Far
Rockaways used to be the site of many fancy
waterfront hotels and beach clubs visited by
wealthy New Yorkers before the land eroded.

BEC BRITTAIN

RED HOOK

Bec Brittain, who trained as an architect
and as an industrial designer, bases many
of her works on crystals, which she finds
to have both the physical structure and
conceptual attributes perfect for making
lighting fixtures. Her SHY light fixture
hangs from a single cord, extending out in
three dimensions while retaining an organic,
linear quality. The LED tubes are fused with
the brass armature to define the shape and
balance bright light with warm metal tones.
The fixture is built out of modular hardware
and so can be configured to fit different
spaces, again referencing crystal variations
based on the same structural foundation.

UHURU

/

RED HOOK

The design team Uhuru believes that if you create good design with a narrative, then people are less likely to throw it away. This ties well to their practice of using only reclaimed materials in their furniture, some of it salvaged from famous locations such as the Coney Island Boardwalk. As the 1940s ipe wood was being taken up to make way for a renovated boardwalk, Uhuru brought loads of it back to their shop in Red Hook and started making a line of furniture out of it. The Cyclone Lounger comes from the Coney Island line. Not only did the piece physically grow out of the historic place; its design also tells the story of its origin through the undulating curve of its seat and the Cyclonesque base made of laser-cut metal, which has been powder-coated white.

FORT STANDARD

/

RED HOOK

Gregory Buntain and Ian Collings made their first Column coffee table—a sturdy square marble slab with turned white-oak legs—based on the design requirements of a friend and client. Now bending and turning wood, stone, and glass are practices the duo, known as Fort Standard, regularly apply to their work. The Counterweight floor lamp was inspired by vintage molds at Flickinger Glassworks downstairs from their shop. They wanted to create a lighting fixture using kiln-formed glass, and although these objects often are more craft-oriented, Buntain and Collings sought to use the technique to make something elegant and modern. The cylindrical mold they settled on informed the wood components of the lamp, which they steam-bent to create a simple, organic stem.

"Brooklyn offers a means to understand possibilities for working with materials," says Collings. "If we were in another city, all of that work with the glassmakers would have been a phone conversation. There's an accessibility here that offers a lot to us. Just knowing it was there was a big inspiration."

SELECTED DESIGN AND FABRICATION SOURCES

RENOVATION

2ND STREET (page 28)
ARCHITECT:
Abelow Sherman Architects, LLC
212-627-8866
www.abelowsherman.com

CONTRACTOR:
Top Drawer Construction Corp.
212-254-2333
www.topdrawerconstruction.com
debi@topdrawerconstruction

KITCHEN CABINETRY:
Henry Built
212-966-5797
www.henrybuilt.com
inquiries@henrybuilt.com

PROSPECT PLACE GARDEN (page 38)
ARCHITECT, KITCHEN:
Baird Architects
212-334-2499
www.bairdarchitects.com

FLOORS:
Norwegian Wood Floors
718-218-8880
www.norwegianwoodfloors.com
info@norwegianwoodfloors.com

GARDEN CONTRACTOR:
JSeigleBuilt
845-489-0613
www.jseiglebuilt.com
info@jseiglebuilt.com

LANDSCAPE DESIGNER:
Foras Studio, LLC
347-750-6496
www.foras-studio.com
info@foras-studio.com

STAINLESS-STEEL CABINETRY:
Marlo Manufacturing, Inc.
973-423-0226
www.marlomfg.com

STONE FIREPLACE:
New York Quarries, Inc.
518-756-3138
www.alcovestone.com
info@alcovestone.com

3RD STREET (page 46)
ARCHITECT:
Fogarty Finger Architecture Interiors
212-966-7485
www.fogartyfinger.com
info@fogartyfinger.com

CONTRACTOR:
Kudos
212-564-4711
www.kudosconstruction.com

DINING ROOM TABLE:
Mira Nakashima
215-862-2272
www.nakashimawoodworker.com
info@nakashimawoodworker.com

DINING CHAIRS AND BAR TABLE:
Eric Manigian Studio
646-470-8733
www.ericmanigian.com
info@ericmanigian.com

FURNITURE:
Vladimir Kagan
www.vladimirkagan.com

RUGS:
Kea Carpets and Kilims
718-222-8087
www.keacarpetsandkilims.com
info@keacarpetsandkilims.com

Rug Art
212-207-8211
www.rug-art.net
info@rug-art.net

WALLPAPER:
Sarah Morris
www.artwareeditions.com

Maharam
www.maharam.com
clientservices@maharam.com

CHEEVER PLACE (page 56)
ARCHITECT AND CONSTRUCTION MANAGER:
Leone Design Studio
718-243-9088
www.leonedesignstudio.com
info@leonedesignstudio.com

CARPENTRY:
JPO Contracting
631-757-4400

FINISH CARPENTRY:
Rose and Stone Construction
917-328-9864
david@rosestoneconstruction.com

MILLWORK:
Anthony Dalo Woodworking
718-418-9001
www.adalowood.com
anthony@adalowood.com

STONEWORK:
Nitti Marble
718-539-8901

CLINTON STREET ROOFTOP GARDEN
(page 62)
CONTRACTOR:
Showcase Construction
718-448-8955

IRRIGATION:
Potenzano Irrigation & Lighting, Inc.
888-860-7400
www.potenzanoirrigation.com

LANDSCAPE DESIGNER:
xs space
917-566-0571
www.xsspace.com

PROSPECT PARK WEST (page 66)
DINING ROOM WALL TREATMENT:
Cavanaugh Wall Solutions, Inc.
866-783-6483
www.cavanaugh-wall.com

GLASS:
Bendheim
212-226-6370
www.bendheim.com

INTERIOR DESIGN:
Leyden Lewis Design Studio
718-302-0822
www.leydenlewis.com
contactus@leydenlewis.com

LEATHER FLOOR:
Edelman Leather
www.edelmanleather.com

LIVING ROOM RUG:
Carini Lang
646-613-0497
www.carinilang.com

POCKET DOORS:
Face Design + Fabrication
718-486-8288
www.facedesign.com

MIKE D'S TOWNHOUSE (page 72)
ARCHITECT:
Bouratoglou Architect, PC
718-783-7848
www.barchpc.com
info@barchpc.com

CONTRACTOR:
Urban Builders
212-352-3290
www.urbanbuildersnyc.com
urbanbuilders@mac.com

DINING TABLE:
Chris Lehrecke
845-868-1674
www.chrislehrecke.com
info@chrislehrecke.com

INTERIOR DESIGN:
Paula Rodriguez
646-256-8560
paularballve@me.com

KITCHEN AND DINING SHELVES:
ESP Metal Crafts
718-381-2443
www.espmetalcrafts.com
sales@espmetalcrafts.com

RUGS:
Breuckelen Berber
718-576-3188
www.breuckelenberber.com
info@breuckelenberber.com

WALLPAPER DESIGN (BROOKLYN TOILE):
Revolver New York
www.revolvernewyork.com
Fabricated by Flavor Paper

WOOD FINISHING:
Southslope Woodworks
718-832-1058
www.southslopewoodworks.com
info@southslopewoodworks.com

BELLOCQ TEA ATELIER (page 82)
104 West Street
800-495-5416
www.bellocq.com
inquiries@bellocq.com

DESIGN AND BUILD:
SAAW, Inc.
215-636-0677
www.saaw.com
sstewart@saaw.com

THE INVISIBLE DOG ART CENTER (page 86)
51 Bergen Street
347-560-3641
www.theinvisibledog.org
lucien@theinvisibledog.org

BELT BUCKLE CHANDELIER:
Steven and William Ladd
646-238-7009
www.stevenandwilliam.com
info@stevenandwilliam.com

ELEVATOR SHAFT INSTALLATION:
Giuseppe Stampone
www.giuseppestampone.com

LINCOLN PLACE (page 90)
DESIGN AND BUILD:
The Brooklyn Home Company
718-715-0418
www.thebrooklynhomecompany.com
chad@brooklynhomecompany.com

CLINTON STREET (page 94)
ARCHITECT:
BArC Studio
646-255-2734
www.barcstudio.com
info@barcstudio.com

LIGHTING:
Doug Newton
bkhandbuilt@gmail.com

RUCOLA (page 102)
190 Dean Street
718-576-3209
www.rucolabrooklyn.com

DESIGN AND BUILD:
Uhuru Design
718-855-6519
www.uhurudesign.com
info@uhurudesign.com

FURNITURE:
Zaborski Emporium and Architectural
Salvage
845-338-6465
www.stanthejunkman.com
sandyballa@verizon.net

METAL TABLE BASES, CRATE WALL:
Fourth State, LLC
718-599-3223
www.4thstatemetals.com
4thstatemetals@verizon.net

WOOD ELEMENTS AND RECLAIMED OAK:
Circle On Dot Woodworks, LLC
718-855-7627

WASHINGTON AVENUE (page 106)
DESIGN AND BUILD:
Nightwood
718-596-1545
www.nightwoodny.com
info@nightwoodny.com

INTERIOR PAINTING:
Fernando Emilio Lucas
347-528-8532
www.flucasconstruction.com
lucasd6@verizon.net

LIGHTING AND METALWORK:
Doug Newton
bkhandbuilt@gmail.com

THE WYTHE HOTEL (page 112)
80 Wythe Avenue
718-460-8000
www.wythehotel.com
hello@wythehotel.com

ARCHITECT:
Morris Adjmi Architects/MA
212-982-2020
www.ma.com
info@ma.com

BEDS:
DHWWD
347-599-1690
www.dhwwd.com
info@dhwwd.com

HOTEL SIGN:
Tom Fruin
www.tomfruin.com
tom@tomfruin.com

LOBBY DESIGN AND LIGHTING:
Workstead
401-573-3023
www.workstead.com
robert@workstead.com

SIDE TABLES AND DESKS:
SAW
917-892-5895
www.SAWhome.com

WALLPAPER DESIGN:
Dan Funderburgh, LLC
347-683-4250
www.danfunderburgh.com
danfunderburgh@gmail.com
Fabricated by Flavor Paper

REYNARD (page 116)
80 Wythe Avenue
718-460-8004
www.wythehotel.com/dining
/restaurant/

LIGHTING:
Works Manufacturing
917-723-1960
www.worksmfg.com
info@worksmfg.com

PAINTING:
3 Fingers Painting, Inc.
646-512-3510
www.3fingerspainting.com
threefingers@me.com

TILING:
Taggios Brothers
917-807-4376

RESTORATION

HANCOCK STREET (page 120)
ARCHITECTURAL SALVAGE, DOORS,
FIREPLACE SURROUNDS, STAINED
GLASS, HARDWARE:
Eddie's Salvage Shop
224 Greene Avenue

DOOR RESTORATION:
Tamer Restoration and Refinishing
718-855-9530
www.tamerandtamer.com
info@tamerandtamer.com

GLASS RESTORERS:
Bear Glass
718-832-3604
www.bearglass.com
info@bearglass.com

KITCHEN WOOD MOLDINGS, CABINETS,
WAINSCOTING:
Dyke's Lumber, in Brooklyn
718-624-3350
www.dykeslumber.com

MARBLE COUNTERS AND BATHROOM:
Key Tile and Stone
718-832-2232
newkeytile@yahoo.com

ALBEMARLE ROAD (page 132)
ARCHITECT:
Kelley/Hemmerly Architecture and Design
718-624-8390

CONTRACTOR:
Square Indigo, Inc.
718-625-3086
www.squareindigo.com

ELECTRICAL:
Laredo Electric
718-227-6607

FLOORS:
Anderson Flooring Co.
718-804-7890

FORT GREENE PARK (page 140)
www.nycgovparks.org/parks
/FortGreenePark

WILLOW STREET (page 140)
ARCHITECT:
Joseph Vance Architects
718-383-1278
www.josephvancearchitects.com
email@jvarchitects.com

CEILING AND WALL PAINTING:
Finished Surface
917-622-7985
www.finishedsurface.com
info@finishedsurface.com

CONTRACTOR:
ABR Construction
www.abrconstruction.com
mailbox@abrconstruction.com

DINING ROOM TABLE WOODWORK AND
FINISHING:
Tamer Restoration and Refinishing
718-855-9530
www.tamerandtamer.com
info@tamerandtamer.com

INTERIOR DESIGN:
Janet Liles Interior Design
718-490-4999
www.janetliles.com

MILLWORK:
Engberg Design and Development
718-875-1685
www.engberg-design.com
ian@engberg-design.com

JANE'S CAROUSEL (page 156)
Brooklyn Bridge Park
Dock Street
718-222-2502
www.janescarousel.com

GLASS, MIRROR, AND SCULPTURAL WORK:
Fiona Westphal
347-495-7652
www.fionawestphal.com

PRIMARY PAINT:
T.J. Ronan Paint Corp.
718-292-1100
www.ronanpaints.com
info@ronanpaints.com

SHELTER ARCHITECT:
Ateliers Jean Nouvel
+33 1 49 23 83 83
www.jeannouvel.com
info@jeannouvel.fr

INNOVATION

ROBERTA'S (page 164)
261 Moore Street
718-417-1118
www.robertaspizza.com

BLANCA (page 170)
261 Moore Street
347-799-2807
www.blancanyc.com

DINING SEATS:
Barrett Seats
860-349-3837
www.barrettseats.com

VANDERBILT AVENUE (page 172)
ARCHITECT:
O'Neill McVoy Architects
347-834-5931
www.oneillmcvoy.com

ARCHITECT OF RECORD:
Joshua Pulver
212-845-9611
www.apluscny.com

S. 4TH STREET (page 176)
ARCHITECT FOR INITIAL BUILD-OUT:
Standard Architects
718-486-0301
www.standardarchitects.com
info@standardarchitects.com

FURNITURE:
Baxter & Liebchen
718-797-0630
www.baxterliebchen.com

SECOND-FLOOR INTERIOR RENOVATION AND
ROOF GARDEN:
Crawford Practice
www.crawfordpractice.com

SIDNEY PLACE GARDEN (page 182)
LANDSCAPE DESIGNER:
dlandstudio
718-624-0244
www.dlandstudio.com
info@dlandstudio.com

**SUNSET PARK MATERIALS RECYCLING
FACILITY** (page 186)
30th Street Pier
ARCHITECT:
Selldorf Architects
212-219-9571
www.selldorf.com
info@selldorf.com

BAM FISHER (page 188)
321 Ashland Place
718-636-4100
www.bam.org/visit/buildings/bam-fisher

ARCHITECT:
H3 Hardy Collaboration Architecture, LLC
212-677-6030
www.h3hc.com
info@h3hc.com

FLAVOR PAPER RESIDENCE (page 192)
ARCHITECT:
Skylab Architecture
503-525-9315
www.skylabarchitecture.com

FLOORS AND CARPETING:
The Floor Group
706-278-7299

MICROPHONE LIGHTS:
Re-Surface
917-669-2642
www.re-surface.net
info@re-surface.net

HOT BIRD (page 200)
546 Clinton Avenue
718-230-5800

ARCHITECTURAL ELEMENTS:
Housewerks
410-685-8047
www.housewerksalvage.com
housewerks@mac.com

BAR STOOLS:
Restoration Hardware, Vintage Toledo
Collection
www.restorationhardware.com

WAVERLY AVENUE (page 204)
ARCHITECT:
David Hecht Architecture, PC
david@davidhechtarchitecture.com

CONTRACTOR:
Lexcore Associates
212-481-7982

FIREPLACE:
Fourth State, LLC
718-599-3223
www.4thstatemetals.com
4thstatemetals@verizon.com

RECLAIMED PINE FLOORING:
Pioneer Millworks
www.pioneermillworks.com

REPLACEMENT HISTORIC DOUBLE-HUNG
WINDOWS:
Jeld-Wen
800-535-3936
www.jeldwen.com

STAIRCASE:
AJ Ironworks
718-237-2642

STONE WORK:
Foro Marble Company
718-852-2322

PACIFIC STREET (page 210)
ARCHITECT:
Delson or Sherman Architects, PC
718-789-2919
www.delsonsherman.com
jeff@delsonsherman.com

BOND STREET VEGETABLE GARDEN
(page 216)
ARCHITECT:
MADE
718-834-0171
www.made-nyc.com
info@made-nyc.com

LANDSCAPE DESIGNER:
Foras Studio, LLC
347-750-6496
www.foras-studio.com
info@foras-studio.com

PLANTING BEDS:
JSeigleBuilt
845-489-0613
www.jseiglebuilt.com
info@jseiglebuilt.com

BROOKLYN BOTANIC GARDEN VISITOR
CENTER (page 218)
1000 Washington Avenue
718-623-7200
www.bbg.org

ARCHITECT:
WEISS/MANFREDI
212-760-9002
www.weissmanfredi.com

CONTRACTOR:
E.W. Howell
212-930-1050

INDUSTRY

BROOKLYN NAVY YARD (page 224)
BLDG 92
63 Flushing Avenue
718-907-5992
www.bldg92.org
info@bldg92.org

Duggal Energy Solutions
212-242-7000
www.duggal.com
info@duggal.com

ARCHITECT:
Beyer Blinder Belle
212-777-7800
www.beyerblinderbelle.com
info@bbbarch.com

workshop/apd
212-273-9712
www.workshopapd.com
info@workshopapd.com

NEW LAB (page 228)
Brooklyn Navy Yard
Building 128
63 Flushing Avenue

ARCHITECT:
Rogers Marvel Architects
212-941-6718
www.rogersmarvel.com
info@rogersmarvel.com

DEVELOPER:
Macro Sea
212-533-1200
www.macro-sea.com
info@macro-sea.com

PROJECT CONSULTANT:
Terreform ONE
617-285-0901
www.terreform.org
info@terreform.org

DESIGNERS IN THEIR STUDIOS

WÜD FURNITURE DESIGN (page 230-231)
718-486-7952
www.wudfurniture.com
corey@wudfurniture.com

ASWOON/SUSAN WOODS (page 232)
718-858-7006
www.aswoon.com
susan@aswoon.com

FERRA DESIGNS (page 232)
718-852-8629
www.ferradesigns.com
info@ferradesigns.com

JASON MILLER/ROLL & HILL (page 233)
718-387-6132
www.rollandhill.com
info@rollandhill.com

MARY WALLIS (page 233)
646-580-8135
www.marywallis.com
info@marywallis.com

KATCH DESIGN CO. (page 234)
718-963-2345
www.katchdesignco.com
pamela@katchdesigncompany.com

NIGHTWOOD (page 234-235)
718-596-1545
www.nightwoodny.com
info@nightwoodny.com

VONNEGUT/KRAFT (page 236)
www.vonnegutkraft.com

EGG COLLECTIVE (page 236-237)
347-889-7594
www.eggcollective.com
info@eggcollective.com

TAKESHI MIYAKAWA (page 238)
718-782-0951
www.tmiyakawadesign.com
tmiyakawadesign@gmail.com

ELASTICCO (page 238)
917-676-0478
www.elasticco.com
info@elasticco.com

FLAVOR PAPER (page 239)
718-422-0230
www.flavorpaper.com
info@flavorleague.com

HIROKO TAKEDA (page 239)
917-676-8329
www.hirokotakeda.com
hiroko@hirokotakeda.com

PELLE (page 240)
718-243-1840
www.pelledesigns.com

DAVID WEEKS (page 240-241)
718-596-7945
info@davidweeksstudio.com
www.davidweeksstudio.com

ESKAYEL (page 242)
347-703-8084
www.eskayel.com
info@eskayel.com

HELLMAN-CHANG (page 242)
212-875-0424
www.hellman-chang.com
designs@hellman-chang.com

GROW HOUSE GROW! (page 243)
770-883-2709
www.growhousegrow.com
info@growhousegrow.com

BEC BRITTAIN (page 243)
347-889-1366
www.becbrittain.com
info@becbrittain.com

UHURU (page 244)
718-855-6519
www.uhurudesign.com

FORT STANDARD (page 244-245)
www.fortstandard.com
info@fortstandard.com

RETAIL AND DESIGN STORES OF NOTE

AREAWARE
212-226-5155
www.areaware.com
diana@areaware.com

BUILD IT GREEN
718-725-8925
www.bignyc.org
gowanus@bignyc.org

FILM BIZ RECYCLING
347-384-2336
www.filmbizrecycling.org
info@filmbizrecycling.org

FUTURE PERFECT
718-599-6278
shop.thefutureperfect.com
hello@thefutureperfect.com

TWO JAKES
718-782-7780
www.twojakes.com
info@twojakes.com

ACKNOWLEDGMENTS

I would like to dedicate this book to Barrett and our little Brooklyn boys, Adlai and Dashiell.

There are many people I would like to thank for their gifts of support, time, effort, and ideas. My greatest thanks go to Jane Creech, friend, collaborator, and agent, without whose spark of an idea this book would not have happened. I am grateful for her work on both putting the book together and getting it out into the world. Thank you to Michel Arnaud for his partnership and for bringing the visual realm of *Design Brooklyn* so exquisitely into focus.

I would like to thank Mike Diamond and Lucas Rubin for providing such excellent introductory material, and Leslie Stoker, Elinor Hutton, and Deb Wood at Abrams for perfecting our project and guiding it to fruition. My thanks to Judy Stanton, executive director of the Brooklyn Heights Association, for leading our team to homes in Brooklyn Heights and other communities through the neighborhood associations. Thank you to Morgan Munsey, who connected us to townhouse renovations in Bedford-Stuyvesant and gave an outstanding historical tour of the neighborhood. I am grateful to Lindsay Barton Barrett and Alex Barrett for introducing us to homes in Carroll Gardens and Clinton Hill, and to Suzanne Spellen, Bob Riegen, and Roz Parr for linking us with homeowners in Crown Heights and Prospect Heights.

Ruth Learnard Goldstein, founding chair of the Fort Greene Park Conservancy, provided all of the fascinating history and detail behind the renovation of Fort Greene Park. BNYDC President Andrew Kimball and Daniella Romano of BLDG 92 were instrumental in our gathering of information, access, and understanding of the extraordinary transformation that is taking place in the Brooklyn Navy Yard.

Thank you to stylist Heather Greene, who generously gave her time to help set up so many of the shots that appear in this book.

All of the design stories presented here were made possible by the hospitality of the homeowners who opened their houses to us, the architects who made these visions a reality, and the designers who invited us into their remarkably creative worlds. Thank you.

—ANNE HELLMAN

It is often said, it takes a team to create a visual book. It's true!

First, I would like to thank my coauthor, Anne Hellman, who graciously introduced me to many wonderful Brooklyn neighborhoods and who wrote each story with skillful care. Anne's organization and research made my job a pleasure.

Lucas Rubin was an important part of our team. His knowledge and enthusiasm for Brooklyn's history helped to set the tone.

I am very grateful to everyone who has made the creation of *Design Brooklyn* such an inspiring experience. Homeowners, architects, and designers generously opened their homes and studios to us, shared their ideas, and gave us leads to other interesting projects.

Many conversations with Brooklynites Chris McVoy and Beth O'Neill led to significant finds. Other friends, such as Gene Albertelli, Corinne Takasaki, and Elena Muldoon, provided links to important connections. I learned much from Lisa Mann and Holly Sumner, who guided us to some exciting locations. Thanks also to my friend Joel Avirom, a Brooklyn native, who gave me valuable insights into the borough.

A special thanks to our publisher, Leslie Stoker, who believed in the book from the very beginning and encouraged its growth. Thank you to Elinor Hutton and Deb Wood, who worked with us to hone and craft a mountain of images and develop an exciting book.

My thanks to my longtime assistant, Pawel Kaminski, a talented photographer in his own right, and Zoe Lind van't Hof, who made sure all of our shoots ran seamlessly.

Lastly, I would like to thank Jane. We met working on beautiful books, and I am glad our association became more than I ever imagined.

—MICHEL ARNAUD

ANNE HELLMAN is a Brooklyn-based writer and editor. She is the coauthor of *LogoLounge 7* (Rockport Publishers, 2012) and *Designers on Design: Joël Desgrippes and Marc Gobé on the Emotional Brand Experience* (Rockport Publishers, 2007). In June 2011, she and her husband completed the renovation of a four-story Greek Revival townhouse in Cobble Hill, where they live with their two sons.

MICHEL ARNAUD is an internationally recognized photographer, having worked exclusively for publications such as *Vogue, House & Garden, Harper's Bazaar, Town & Country, InStyle,* and *Architectural Digest.* He is also the coauthor of *Nashville: Pilgrims of Guitar Town* (STC, 2000) and principal photographer for twelve design and lifestyle books, including *All-American: The Exuberant Style of William Diamond and Anthony Baratta* (Pointed Leaf Press, 2009), *Mr. Color: The Greenbrier and Other Decorating Adventures* (Shannongrove Press, 2011), and *Elegant Rooms That Work: Fantasy and Function in Interior Design* (Rizzoli, 2013). Having lived in Paris and London, Arnaud now divides his time between New York City and Chatham, New York.

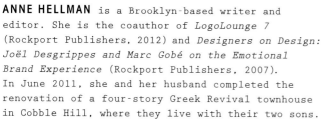

Published in 2013 by Stewart, Tabori & Chang
An imprint of ABRAMS

Library of Congress Control Number: 2013935966
ISBN: 978-1-61769-052-5

Editor: Elinor Hutton
Designer: Deb Wood
Production Manager: True Sims

Printed and bound in China

10 9 8 7 6 5 4 3 2 1

THE ART OF BOOKS SINCE 1949
115 West 18th Street
New York, NY 10011
www.abramsbooks.com